FLUTE BOOK 1

for Band

COMPREHENSIVE BAND METHOD

TIM LAUTZENHEISER • JOHN HIGGINS • CHARLES MENGHINI
PAUL LAVENDER • TOM C. RHODES • DON BIERSCHENK

Band is...

M aking music with a family of lifelong friends.

U nderstanding how commitment and dedication lead to success.

S haring the joy and rewards of working together.

I ndividuals who develop self-confidence.

C reativity—expressing yourself in a universal language.

Band is...**MUSIC!**

Strike up the band,
Tim Lautzenheiser

HISTORY OF THE FLUTE

Flutes were known to exist in ancient civilizations. Over the years, they have been made of wood or metal. Early flutes, such as recorders, are played pointing forward. The other type of flute, called a transverse flute until the mid-1800s, is played to the side.

In 1847, Theobald Boehm designed the modern flute. This flute is capable of playing with more volume than older flutes. The keys Mr. Boehm added also allow the instrument to play a full chromatic scale, and help it to play better in tune.

The flute family includes the C Flute (the most common), C Piccolo, Alto and Bass Flutes. As the highest pitched members of the concert band, marching band and orchestra, flutes play melodies, harmonies and solos, and are important members of the woodwind family.

J. S. Bach, Claude Debussy and Ralph Vaughan Williams are important composers who have written music for the flute. Some famous flute performers are Louis Moyse, James Galway, Claire Chase, Jasmine Choi, and Bobbi Humphrey.

To create an account, visit:
www.essentialelementsinteractive.com

Student Activation Code
E1FL-5873-1649-5131

ISBN 979-835012056-4

THE BASICS

Posture

Sit on the edge of your chair, and always keep your:

- Spine straight and tall
- Shoulders back and relaxed
- Feet flat on the floor

Breathing & Airstream

Breathing is a natural thing we all do constantly. To discover the correct airstream to play your instrument:

- Place the palm of your hand near your mouth.
- Inhale deeply through the corners of your mouth, keeping your shoulders steady. Your waist should expand like a balloon.
- Slowly whisper "too" as you gradually exhale air into your palm.

The air you feel is the airstream. It produces sound through the instrument. Your tongue is like a faucet or valve that releases the airstream.

Producing The Essential Tone

Your embouchure *(ahm´-bah-shure)* is your mouth's position on the mouthpiece of the instrument. A good embouchure takes time and effort, so carefully follow these steps for success:

- Hold the closed end of the head joint in your left hand. Cover the open end with the palm of your right hand.
- Rest the embouchure plate on your bottom lip. Center the embouchure hole on the center of your lips. Check by touching the embouchure hole with the tip of your tongue.
- Gently roll the head joint forward so that approximately 1/4 of the embouchure hole is covered by the lower lip.
- Keep upper and lower teeth spaced slightly apart.
- Draw the corners of your mouth straight back and relax your lower lip.
- Make a small opening in the center of your lips. Blow air partly into and partly across the embouchure hole.
- Practice regularly in front of a mirror. Roll the head joint in or out to find the embouchure position that produces your best clear and full tone.

Taking Care Of Your Instrument

Before putting your instrument back in its case after playing, do the following:

- Carefully remove the head joint and shake any water out.
- Put a clean soft cloth on the end of your cleaning rod and swab out the head joint.
- Twist the middle and foot joints apart and draw the cleaning rod through each joint.
- Carefully wipe the outside of each section to keep the finish clean.

MOUTHPIECE WORKOUT

Form your embouchure around the mouthpiece, and take a deep breath without raising your shoulders. Whisper "too" and gradually exhale your full airstream. Strive for an even tone.

REST

REST

See inside front cover for information on accessing instructional videos.

Getting It Together

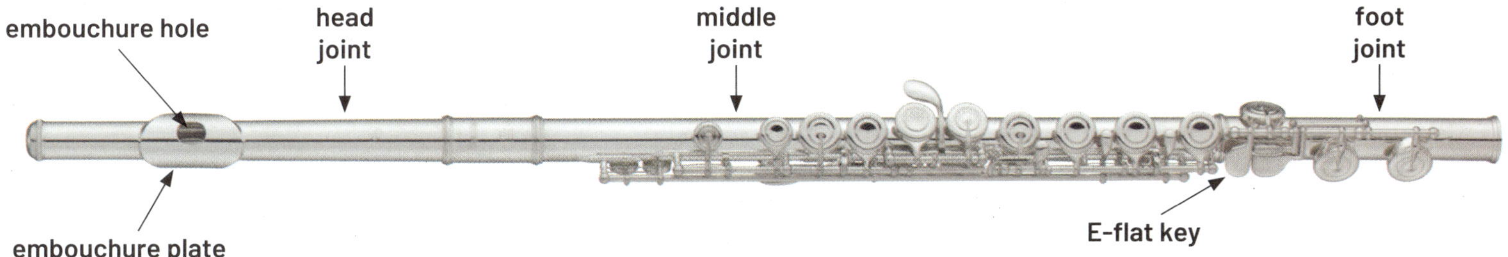

Step 1 Hold the head joint in your left hand and the middle joint in your right hand. Gently twist and insert the head joint into the middle joint. Make sure that the embouchure hole is directly in line with the middle joint's row of keys.

Step 2 Hold the assembled middle joint in your left hand and the foot joint in your right hand. Gently twist and insert the middle joint into the foot joint. The embouchure hole, keys of the middle joint and the long rod on the foot joint should all line up.

Step 3 Rest your left thumb on the underside's long straight key. Keep your wrist straight. Your fingers should arch naturally. Rest your fingertips on the center of the keys.

Step 4 Place the tip of your right thumb on the flute's underside between your first and second fingers. Arch your fingers and rest them lightly on the keys. Put your little finger on the E-flat key.

Step 5 Allow the embouchure plate to press lightly against your lower lip. Hold the flute as shown:

The student shown is a member of the Milwaukee Youth Symphony Orchestra.

READING MUSIC

Identify and draw each of these symbols:

Music Staff

The **music staff** has 5 lines and 4 spaces where notes and rests are written.

Ledger Lines

Ledger lines extend the music staff. Notes on ledger lines can be above or below the staff.

Measures & Bar Lines

Bar lines divide the music staff into **measures**.

Long Tone  To begin, we'll use a special "Long Tone" note. Hold the tone until your teacher tells you to rest. Practice long tones each day to develop your sound.

1. THE FIRST NOTE

Hold each long tone until your teacher tells you to rest.

F

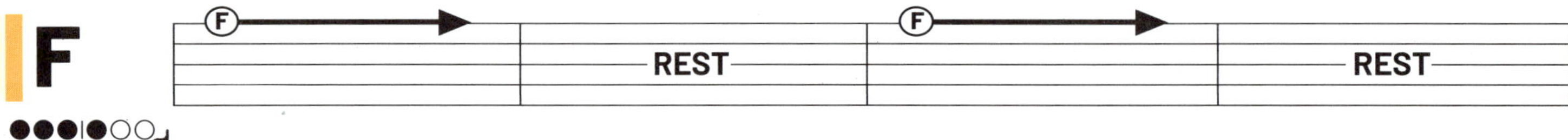

▲ *To play "F," place your fingers on the keys as shown.*

The Beat

The **beat** is the pulse of music, and like your heartbeat it should remain very steady. Counting aloud and foot-tapping help us maintain a steady beat. Tap your foot **down** on each number and **up** on each "&."

One beat = 1 &

↓ ↑

Notes & Rests

Notes tell us how high or low to play by their placement on a line or space of the music staff, and how long to play by their shape. **Rests** tell us to count silent beats.

Quarter Note = 1 beat

Quarter Rest = 1 silent beat

2. COUNT AND PLAY

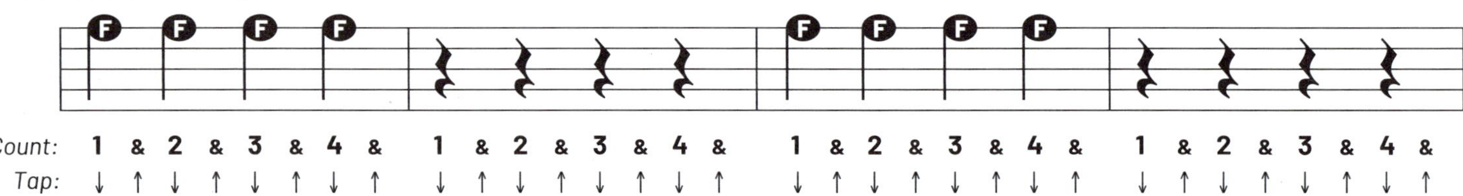

3. A NEW NOTE

Look for the fingering diagram under each new note. This note is "E♭ (E-flat)."

4. TWO'S A TEAM

Count & Tap: 1 & 2 & 3 & 4 & 1 & 2 & 3 & 4 & 1 & 2 & 3 & 4 & 1 & 2 & 3 & 4 &

5. HEADING DOWN

Practice long tones on each new note.

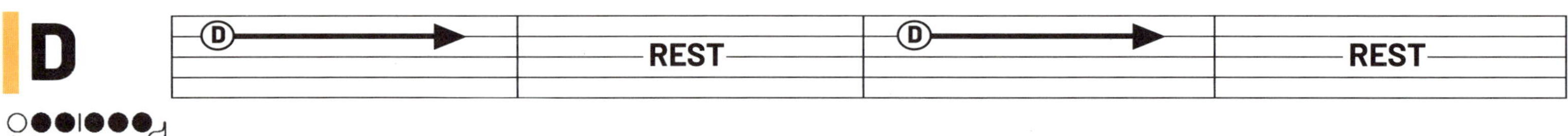

6. MOVING ON UP

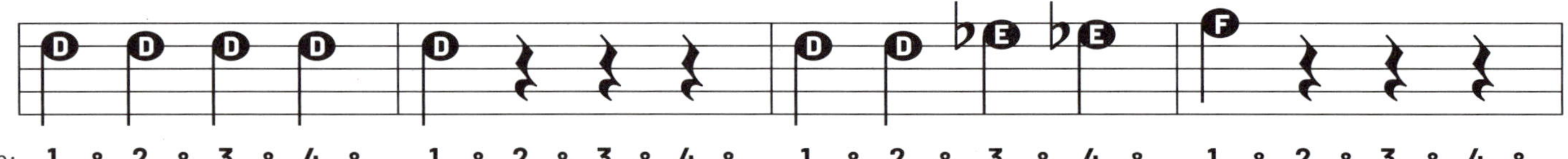

Count & Tap: 1 & 2 & 3 & 4 & 1 & 2 & 3 & 4 & 1 & 2 & 3 & 4 & 1 & 2 & 3 & 4 &

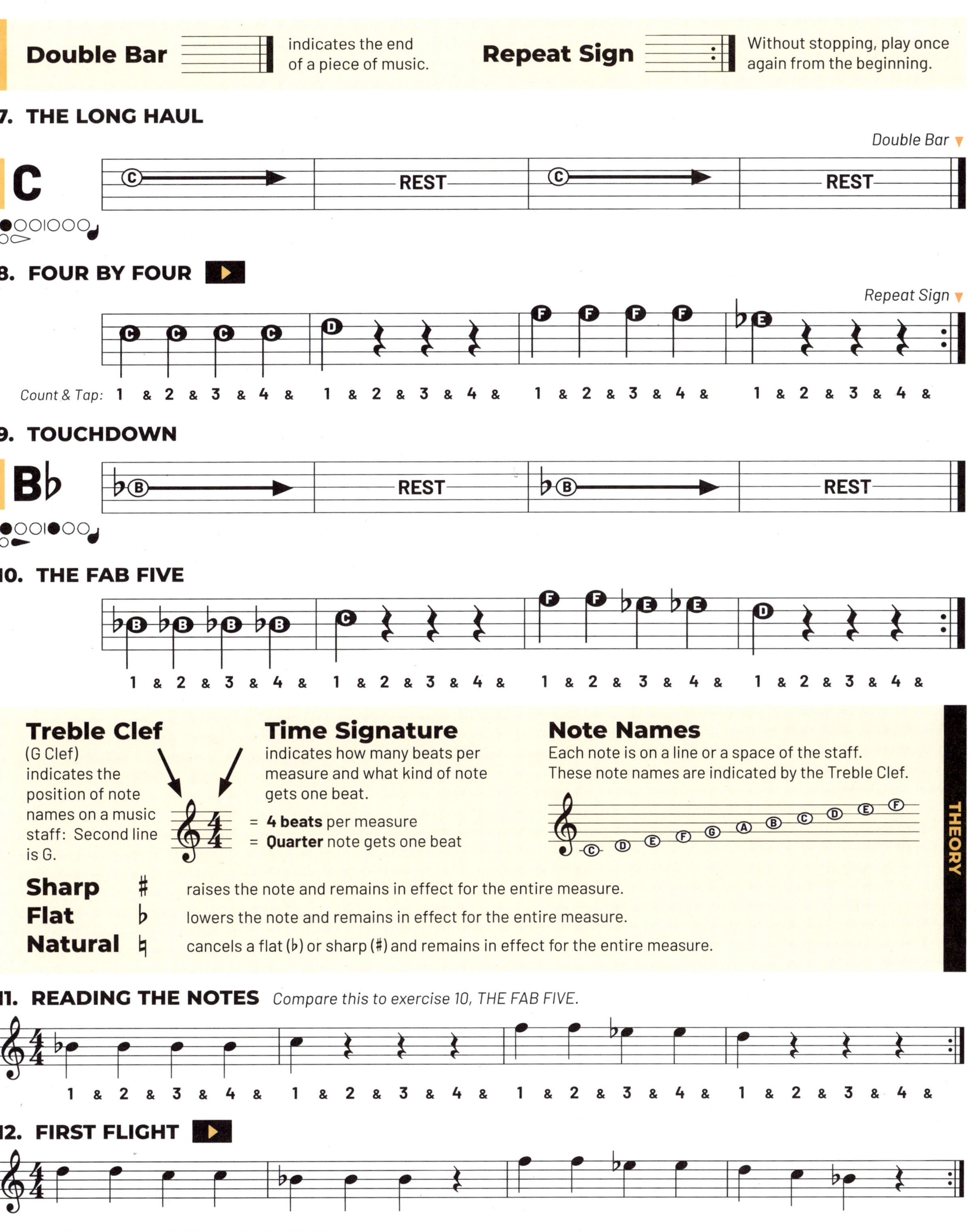

13. ESSENTIAL ELEMENTS QUIZ

Fill in the remaining note names before playing.

B♭ C D ___ ___ ___ ___ ___ ___ ___ ___ ___ ___ ___ ___ ___

Notes In Review

Memorize the fingerings for the notes you've learned:

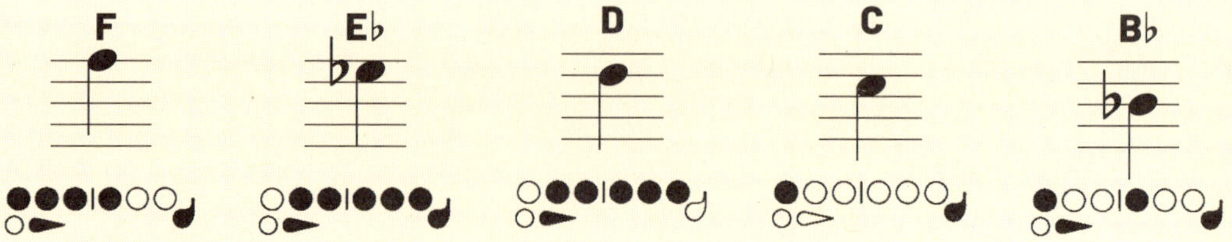

F
E♭
D
C
B♭

14. ROLLING ALONG

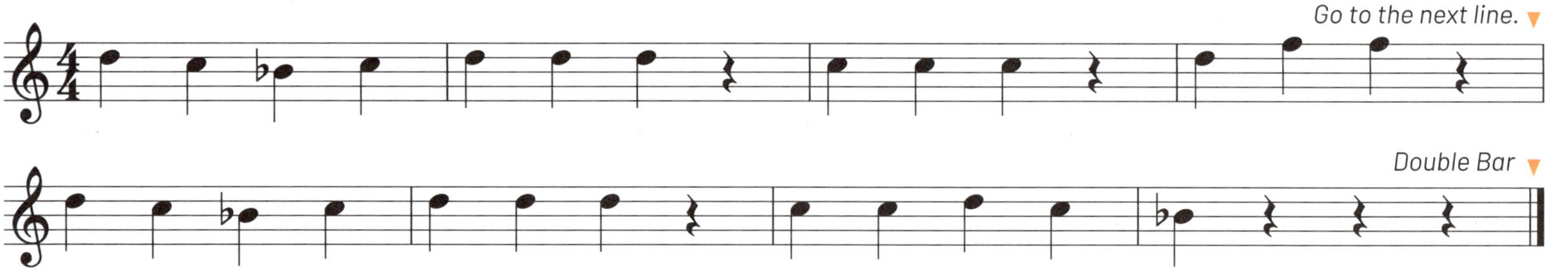

Go to the next line.
Double Bar

Half Note

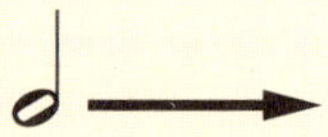

= 2 Beats

1 & 2 &

Half Rest

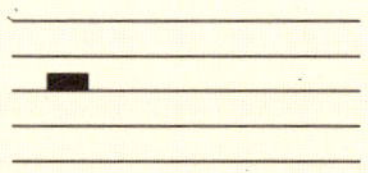

= 2 Silent Beats

1 & 2 &

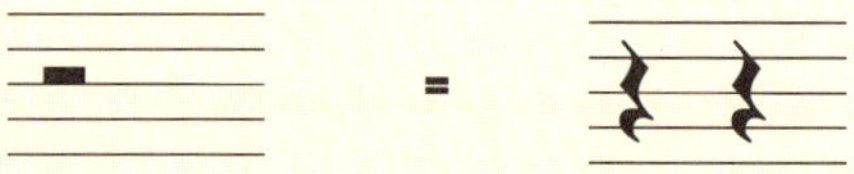

15. RHYTHM RAP *Clap the rhythm while counting and tapping.*

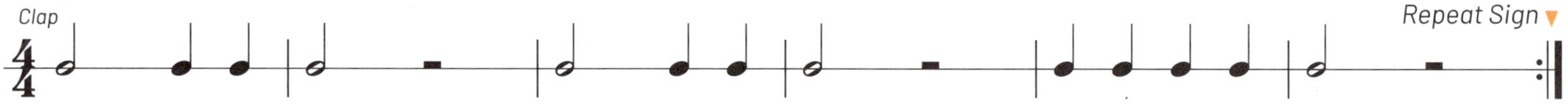

Clap
Repeat Sign

1 & 2 & 3 & 4 & 1 & 2 & 3 & 4 & 1 & 2 & 3 & 4 & 1 & 2 & 3 & 4 & 1 & 2 & 3 & 4 & 1 & 2 & 3 & 4 &

16. THE HALF COUNTS

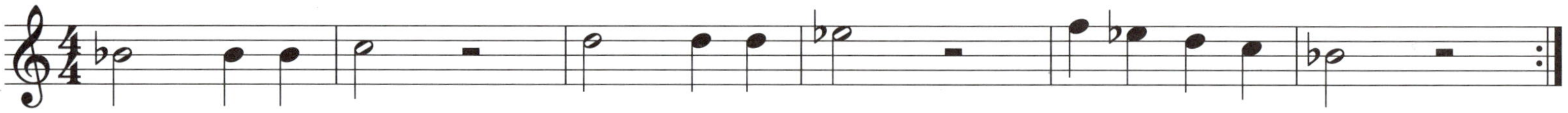

1 & 2 & 3 & 4 & 1 & 2 & 3 & 4 & 1 & 2 & 3 & 4 & 1 & 2 & 3 & 4 & 1 & 2 & 3 & 4 & 1 & 2 & 3 & 4 &

17. HOT CROSS BUNS *Check your embouchure and hand position.*

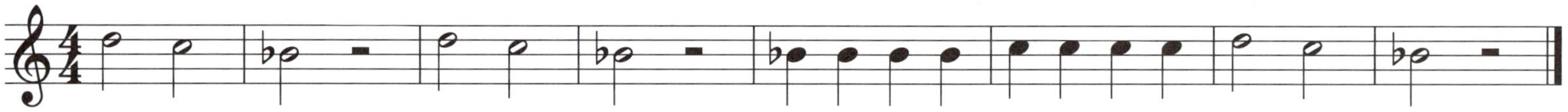

Breath Mark ,

Take a deep breath through your mouth after you play a full-length note.

18. GO TELL AUNT RHODIE

American Folk Song

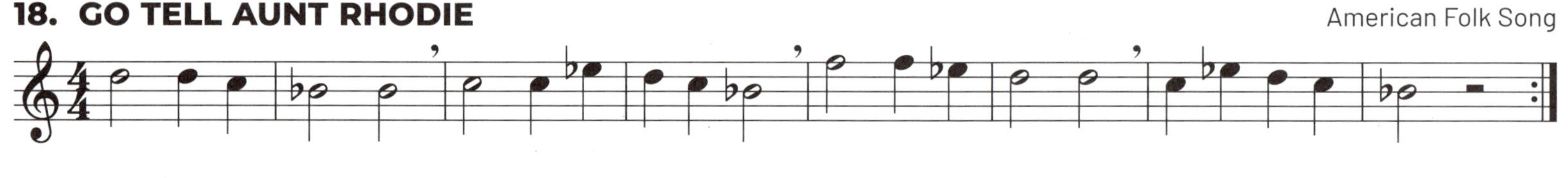

19. ESSENTIAL ELEMENTS QUIZ *Using the note names and rhythms below, draw your notes on the staff before playing.*

E♭ F E♭ D E♭ D C B♭ C D E♭ D E♭

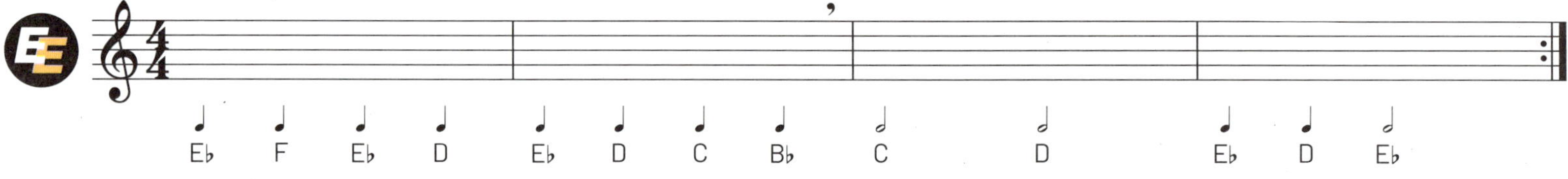

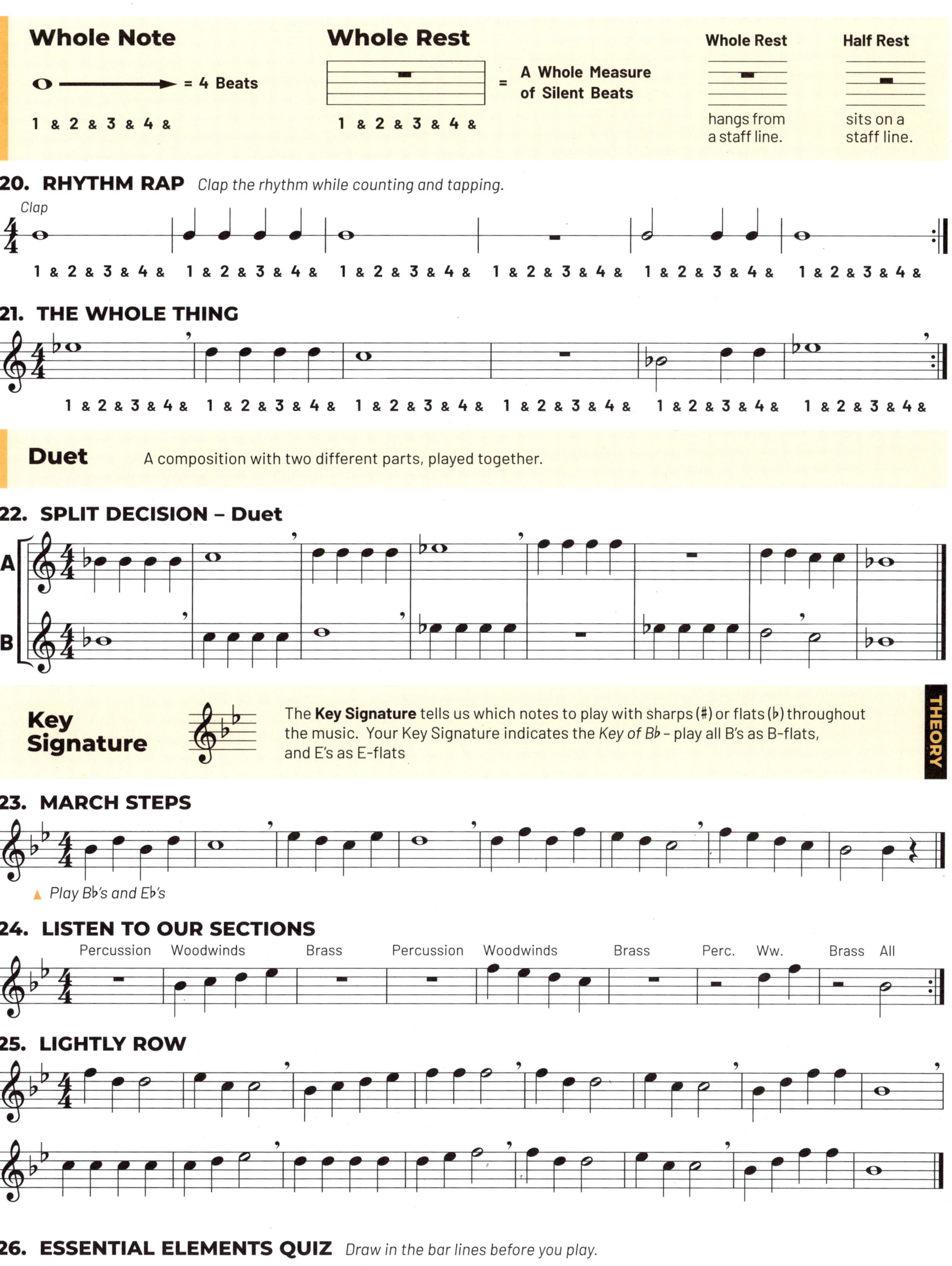
Whole Note
= 4 Beats
1 & 2 & 3 & 4 &
Whole Rest
= A Whole Measure of Silent Beats
1 & 2 & 3 & 4 &
Whole Rest
hangs from a staff line.
Half Rest
sits on a staff line.
20. RHYTHM RAP Clap the rhythm while counting and tapping.
Clap
1 & 2 & 3 & 4 & 1 & 2 & 3 & 4 & 1 & 2 & 3 & 4 & 1 & 2 & 3 & 4 & 1 & 2 & 3 & 4 & 1 & 2 & 3 & 4 &
21. THE WHOLE THING
1 & 2 & 3 & 4 & 1 & 2 & 3 & 4 & 1 & 2 & 3 & 4 & 1 & 2 & 3 & 4 & 1 & 2 & 3 & 4 & 1 & 2 & 3 & 4 &
Duet
A composition with two different parts, played together.
22. SPLIT DECISION – Duet
A
B
Key Signature
The Key Signature tells us which notes to play with sharps (♯) or flats (♭) throughout the music. Your Key Signature indicates the Key of B♭ – play all B's as B-flats, and E's as E-flats
THEORY
23. MARCH STEPS
Play B♭'s and E♭'s
24. LISTEN TO OUR SECTIONS
Percussion
Woodwinds
Brass
Percussion
Woodwinds
Brass
Perc.
Ww.
Brass
All
25. LIGHTLY ROW
26. ESSENTIAL ELEMENTS QUIZ Draw in the bar lines before you play.

Fermata 𝄐 Hold the note (or rest) longer than normal.

27. REACHING HIGHER – New Note

Practice long tones on each new note.

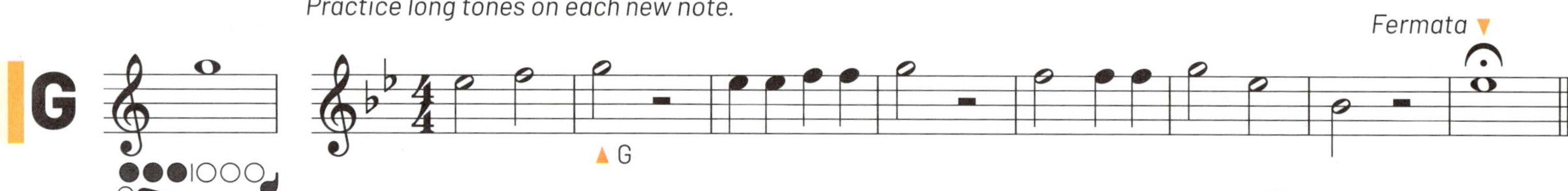

28. AU CLAIRE DE LA LUNE

French Folk Song

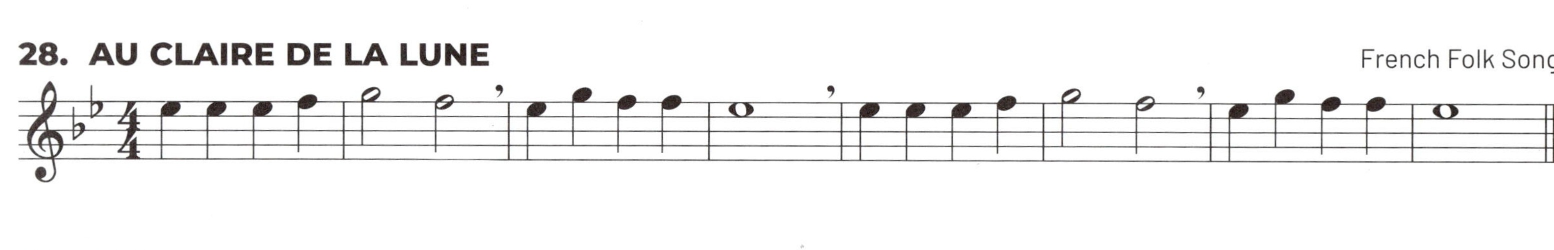

29. REMIX

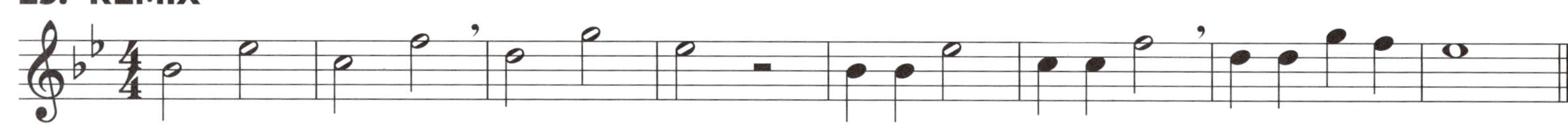

THEORY

Harmony Two or more notes played together. Each combination forms a *chord*.

30. LONDON BRIDGE – Duet

English Folk Song

HISTORY

Austrian composer **Wolfgang Amadeus Mozart** (1756–1791) was a child prodigy who started playing professionally at age six, and lived during the time of the American Revolution. Mozart's music is melodic and imaginative. He wrote more than 600 compositions during his short life, including a piano piece based on the famous song, "Twinkle, Twinkle, Little Star."

31. A MOZART MELODY

Adaptation

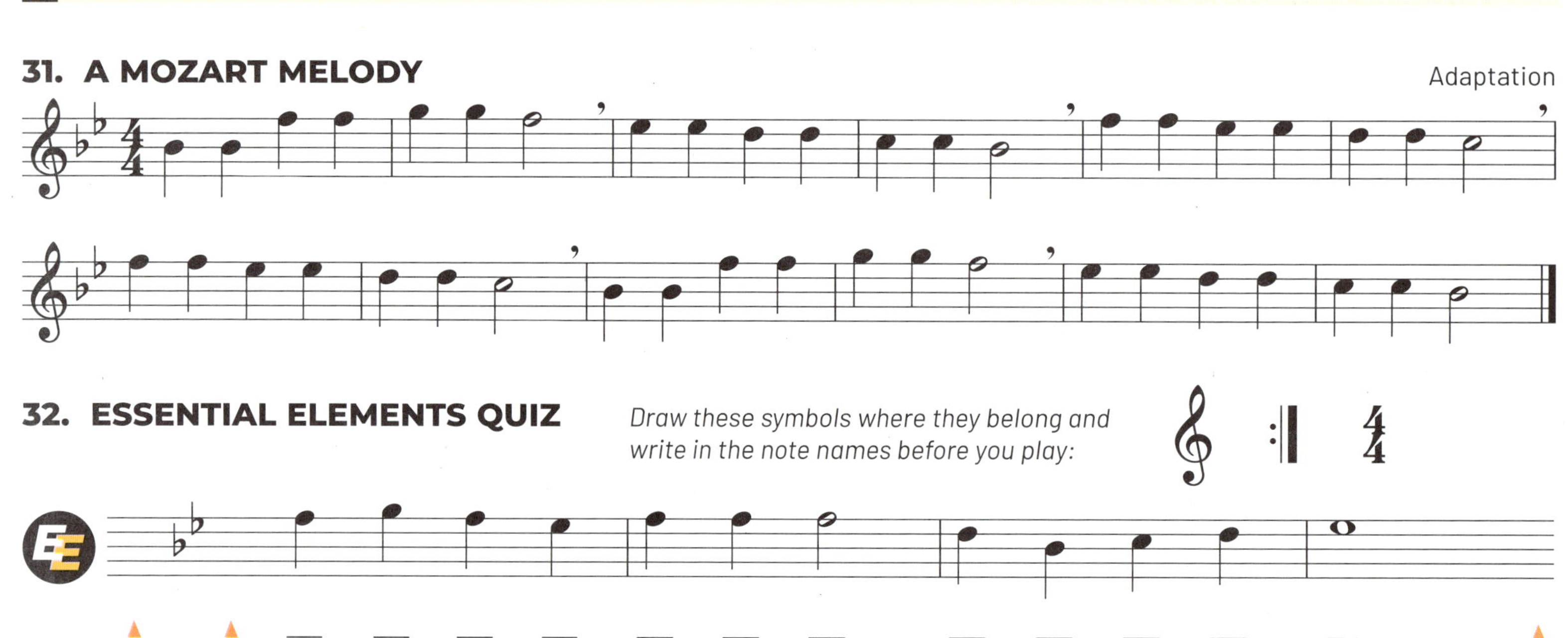

32. ESSENTIAL ELEMENTS QUIZ

Draw these symbols where they belong and write in the note names before you play:

33. DEEP POCKETS – New Note

34. DOODLE ALL DAY

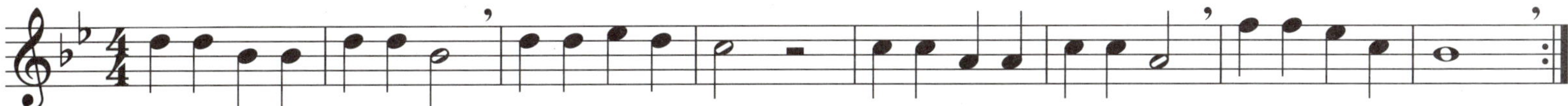

35. JUMP ROPE

Pick-Up Notes One or more notes that come before the first *full* measure. The beats of Pick-Up Notes are subtracted from the last measure.

36. A-TISKET, A-TASKET

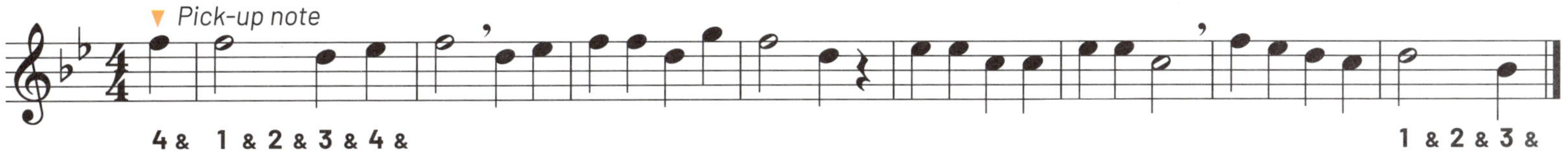

Dynamics ***f*** - *forte* (play loudly) ***mf*** - *mezzo forte* (play moderately loud) ***p*** - *piano* (play softly)
Remember to use full breath support to control your tone at all dynamic levels.

37. LOUD AND SOFT

38. JINGLE BELLS *Keep your fingers close to the keys, curved naturally.*

J. S. Pierpont

39. MY DREYDL *Use full breath support at all dynamic levels.*

Traditional Hanukkah Song

Eighth Notes

1 &

Each Eighth Note = ½ Beat
2 Eighth Notes = 1 Beat
Play on down and up taps.

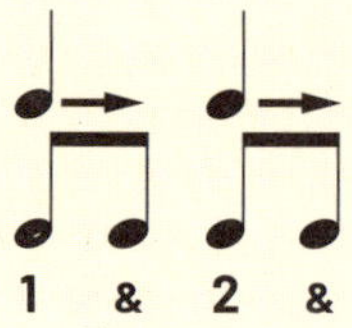

1 & 2 &

Two or more Eighth Notes have a *beam* across the stems.

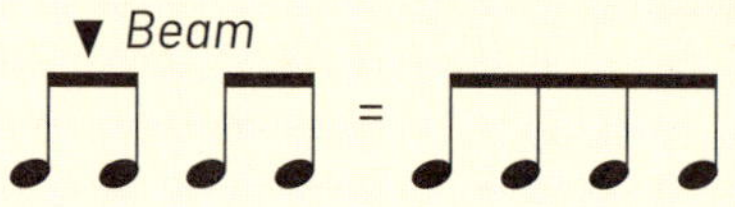

Beam

=

40. RHYTHM RAP *Clap the rhythm while counting and tapping.*

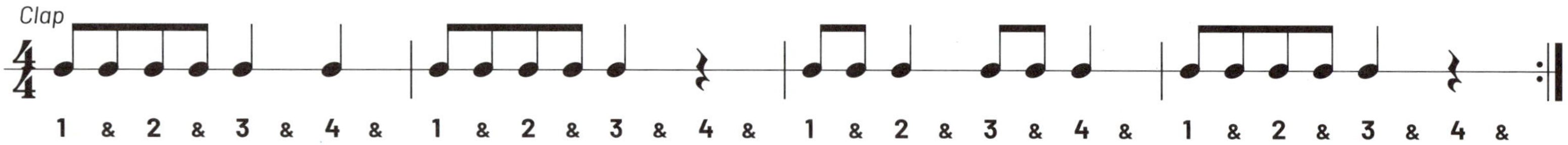

Clap

1 & 2 & 3 & 4 & 1 & 2 & 3 & 4 & 1 & 2 & 3 & 4 & 1 & 2 & 3 & 4 &

41. EIGHTH NOTE JAM

1 & 2 & 3 & 4 & 1 & 2 & 3 & 4 & 1 & 2 & 3 & 4 & 1 & 2 & 3 & 4 &

42. SKIP TO MY LOU

American Folk Song

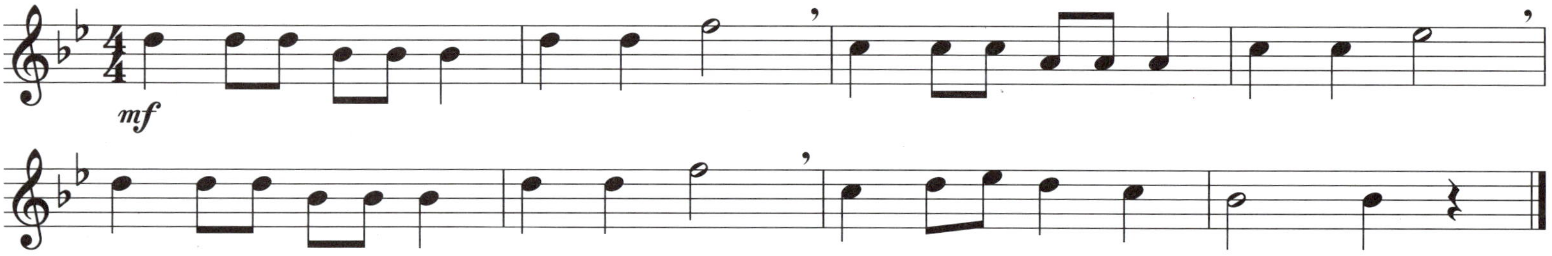

mf

43. LONG, LONG AGO *Good posture improves your sound. Always sit straight and tall.*

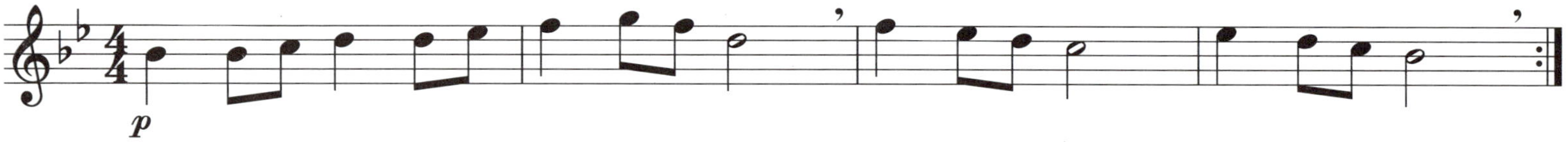

p

44. CANDY MOUNTAIN ROCK

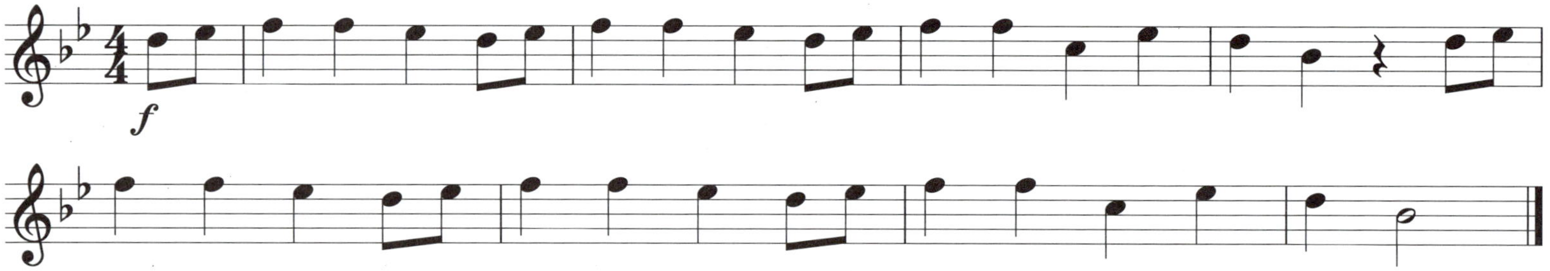

f

HISTORY

Italian composer **Gioachino Rossini** (1792–1868) began composing as a teenager and was very proficient on the piano, viola and horn. He wrote "William Tell" at age 37 as the last of his forty operas, and its familiar theme is still heard today on radio and television.

45. ESSENTIAL ELEMENTS QUIZ – WILLIAM TELL

Gioacchino Rossini

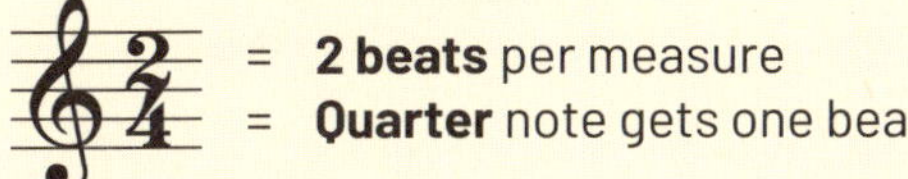

Conducting

Practice conducting this two-beat pattern.

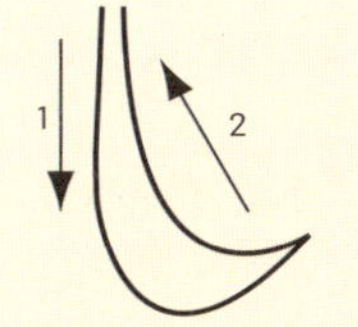

46. RHYTHM RAP

47. TWO BY TWO

Tempo Markings

Tempo is the speed of music. Tempo markings are usually written above the staff, in Italian.
Allegro – Fast tempo **Moderato** – Medium tempo **Andante** – Slower walking tempo

John Philip Sousa

49. HEY, HO! NOBODY'S HOME – New Note

Dynamics

Crescendo (gradually louder) *Decrescendo* or *Diminuendo* (gradually softer)

50. CLAP THE DYNAMICS

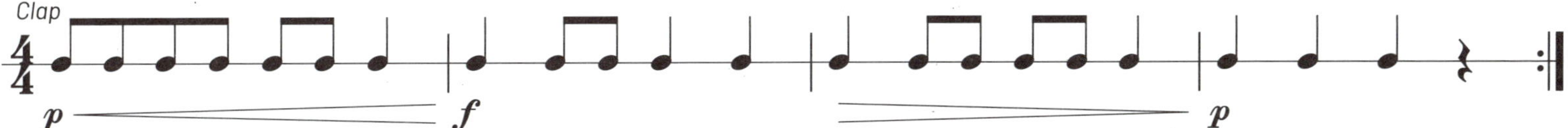

51. PLAY THE DYNAMICS

Looking for some more fun music to play?
See the inside front cover for instructions on accessing recent popular Bonus Songs.

PERFORMANCE SPOTLIGHT

52. PERFORMANCE WARM-UPS

TONE BUILDER

RHYTHM ETUDE

RHYTHM RAP

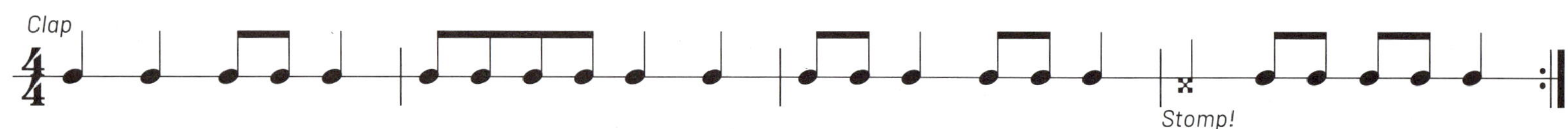

CHORALE

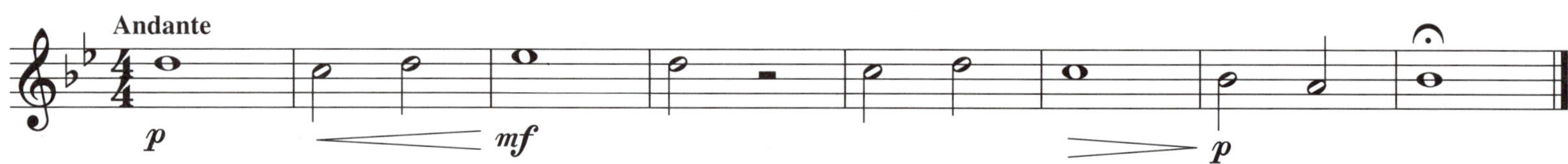

53. AURA LEE – Duet or Band Arrangement

(Part A = Melody, Part B = Harmony)

George R. Poulton

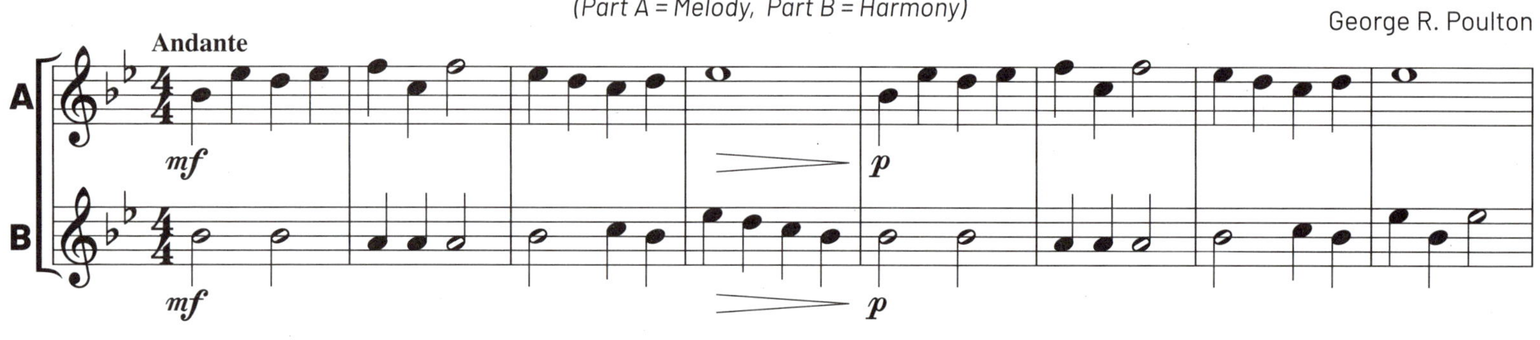

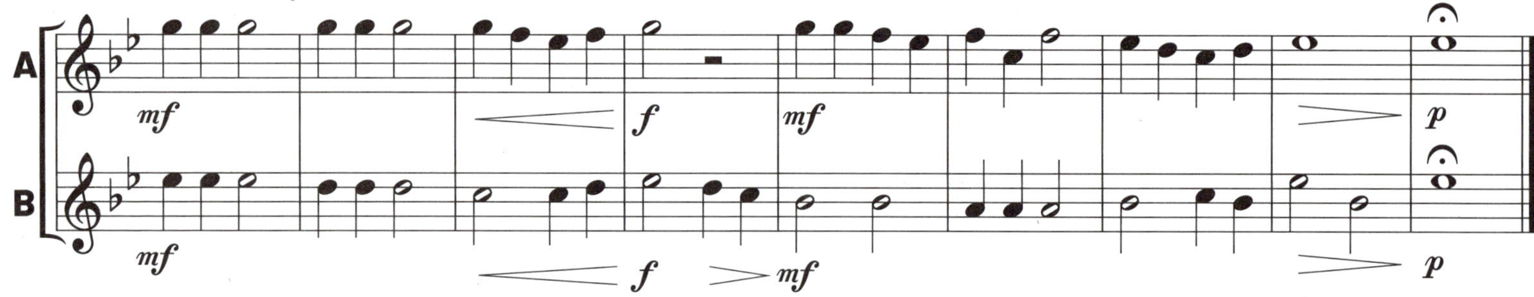

54. FRÈRE JACQUES – Round *(When group A reaches ②, group B begins at ①)*

French Folk Song

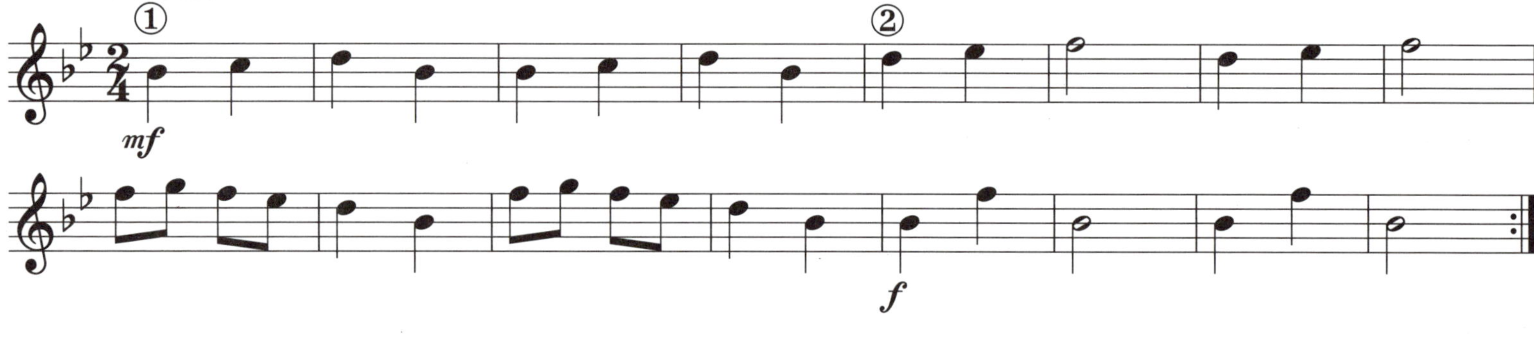

PERFORMANCE SPOTLIGHT

55. WHEN THE SAINTS GO MARCHING IN – Band Arrangement

Arr. by John Higgins

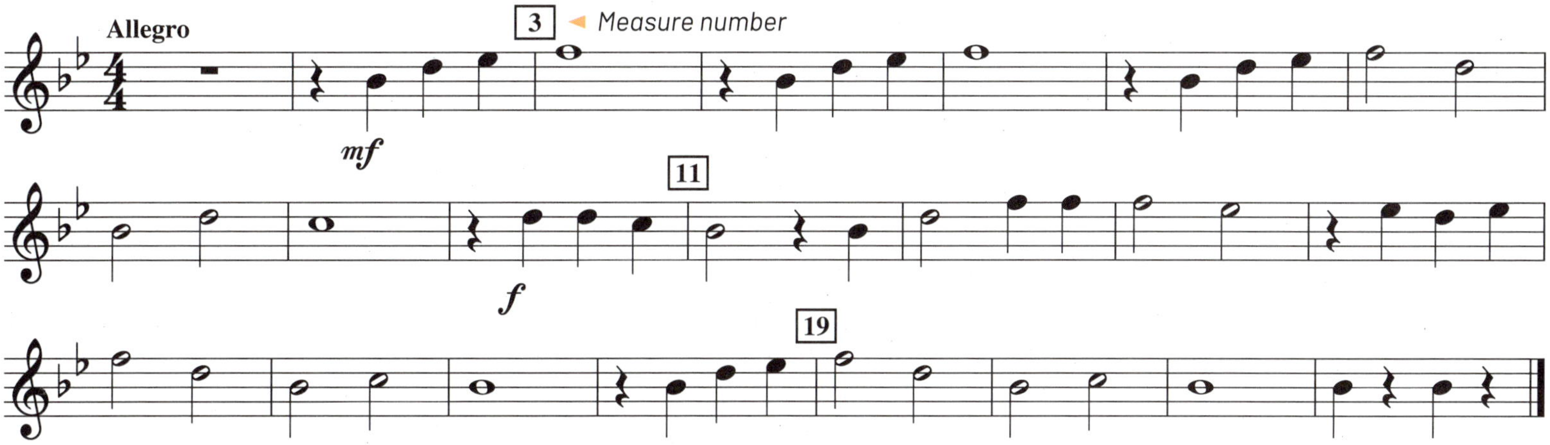

Allegro

3 ◄ *Measure number*

mf

11

f

19

56. OLD MACDONALD HAD A BAND – Section Feature

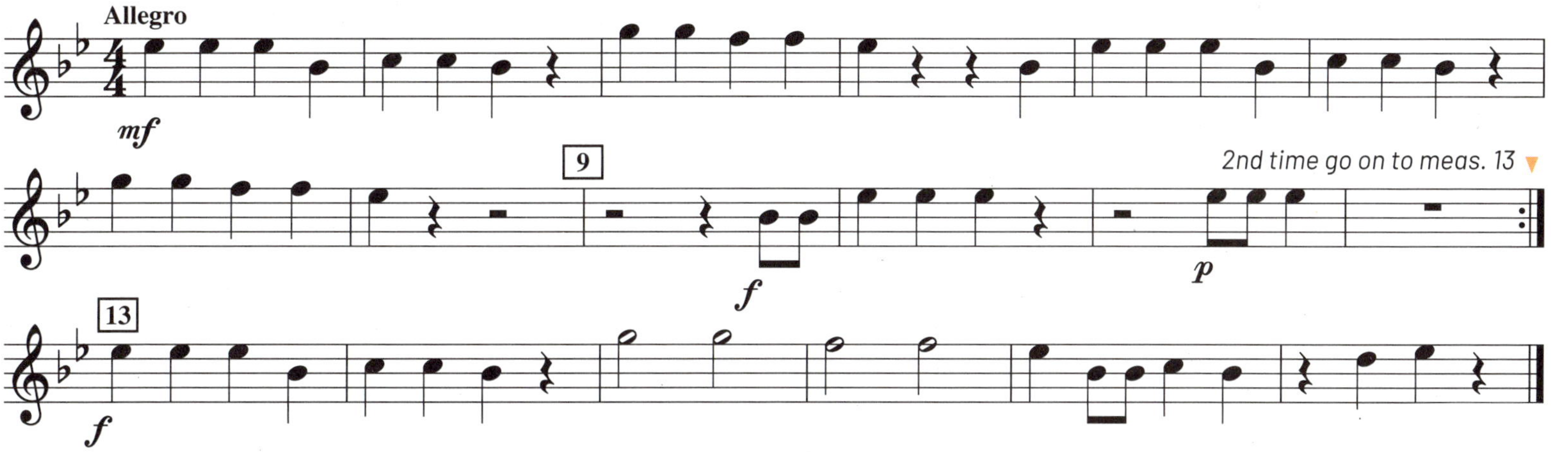

Allegro

mf

9

2nd time go on to meas. 13 ▼

f

p

13

f

57. ODE TO JOY (from Symphony No. 9)

Ludwig van Beethoven
Arr. by John Higgins

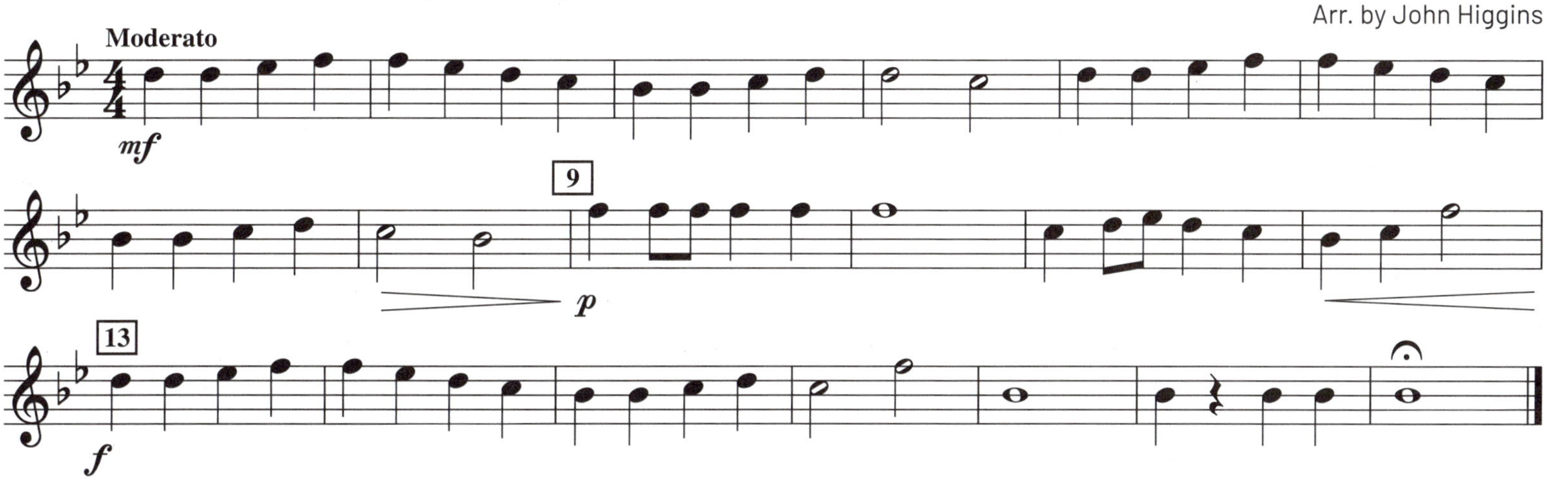

Moderato

mf

9

p

13

f

58. HARD ROCK BLUES – Encore

John Higgins

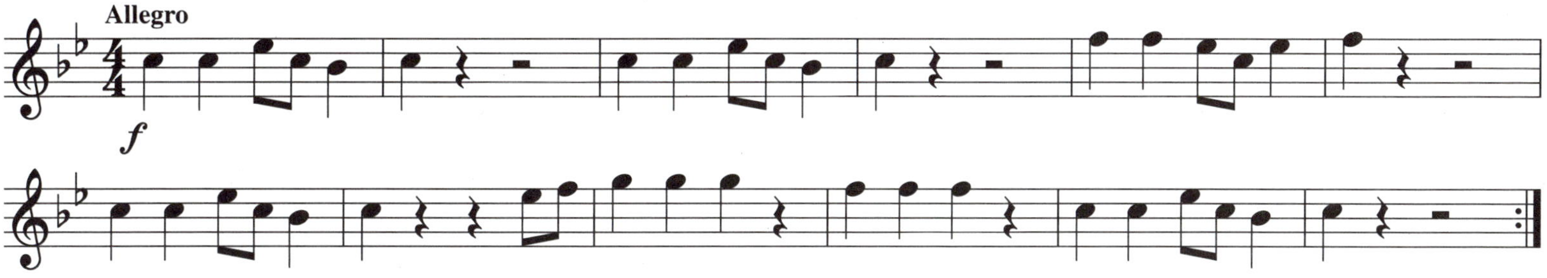

Allegro

f

Tie

A curved line connecting notes of the same pitch.
Play one note for the combined counts of the tied notes.

= 2 Beats

59. FIT TO BE TIED

60. ALOUETTE

French-Canadian Folk Song

Dotted Half Note

= 3 Beats

1 & 2 & 3 &

Dot

A dot adds half the value of the note.

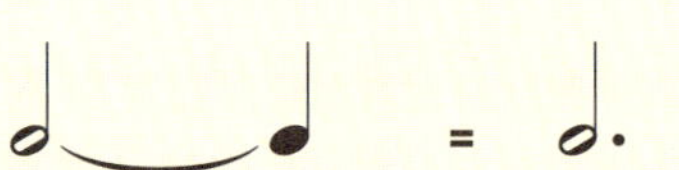

2 beats + 1 beat = 3 beats

61. ALOUETTE – THE SEQUEL

French-Canadian Folk Song

62. IT'S RAINING

63. NEW DIRECTIONS - New Note

To play lower notes, blow softly and direct the airstream lower into the embouchure hole.

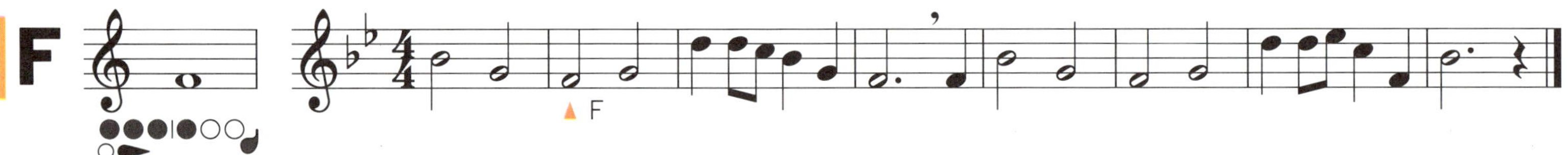

64. THE NOBLES

Always use a full airstream. Keep fingers above the keys, curved naturally.

65. ESSENTIAL ELEMENTS QUIZ

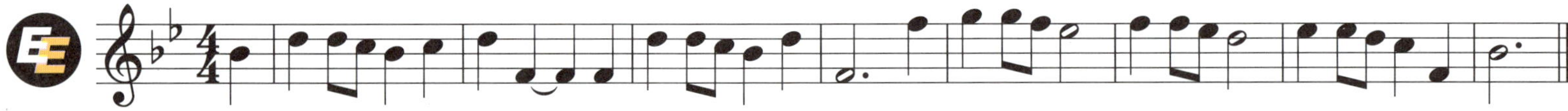

3/4 Time Signature
= 3 beats per measure
= Quarter note gets one beat
Conducting
Practice conducting this three-beat pattern.
1
2
3
THEORY
66. RHYTHM RAP
Clap
1 & 2 & 3 & 1 & 2 & 3 & 1 & 2 & 3 & 1 & 2 & 3 & 1 & 2 & 3 & 1 & 2 & 3 & 1 & 2 & 3 & 1 & 2 & 3 &
67. THREE BEAT JAM
1 & 2 & 3 & 1 & 2 & 3 & 1 & 2 & 3 & 1 & 2 & 3 & 1 & 2 & 3 & 1 & 2 & 3 & 1 & 2 & 3 & 1 & 2 & 3 &
68. BARCAROLLE
Jacques Offenbach
Moderato
mf
HISTORY
Norwegian composer Edvard Grieg (1843–1907) wrote Peer Gynt Suite for a play by Henrik Ibsen in 1875, the year before the telephone was invented by Alexander Graham Bell. "Morning" is a melody from Peer Gynt Suite. Music used in plays, or in films and television, is called incidental music.
69. MORNING (from Peer Gynt)
Edvard Grieg
Andante
p
mf
p
Accent
Emphasize the note.
70. ACCENT YOUR TALENT
Clap
HISTORY
Latin American music has its roots in the African, Native American, Spanish and Portuguese cultures. This diverse music features lively accompaniments by drums and other percussion instruments such as maracas and claves. Music from Latin America continues to influence jazz, classical and popular styles of music. "Chiapanecas" is a popular children's dance and game song.
71. MEXICAN CLAPPING SONG ("Chiapanecas")
Latin American Folk Song
f
72. ESSENTIAL CREATIVITY
Compose your own music for measures 3 and 4 using this rhythm:

THEORY

Accidental

Any sharp, flat or natural sign which appears in the music without being in the key signature is called an **accidental**.

Flat ♭

A **flat** sign lowers the pitch of a note by a half-step. The note A-flat sounds a half-step below A, and all A's become A-flats for the rest of the measure where they occur.

73. HOT MUFFINS – New Note

74. COSSACK DANCE

75. BASIC BLUES – New Note

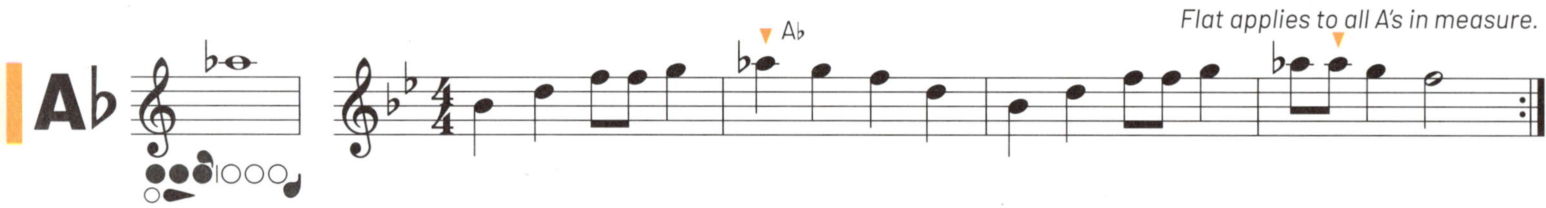

THEORY

New Key Signature

This Key Signature indicates the *Key of E♭* – play all B's as B-flats, all E's as E-flats, and all A's as A-flats.

1st & 2nd Endings

1. 2.

Play through the 1st Ending. Then play the repeated section of music, **skipping** the 1st Ending and playing the 2nd Ending.

76. HIGH FLYING

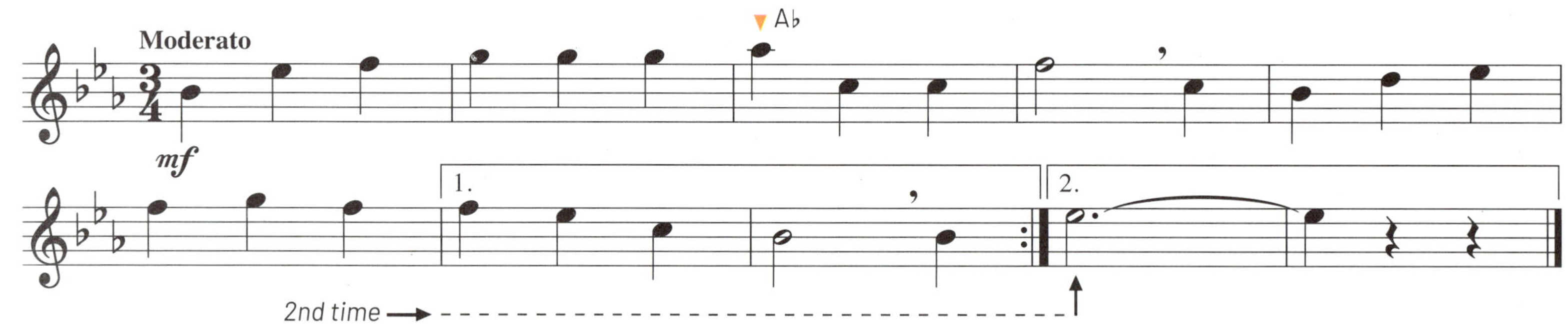

HISTORY

Japanese folk music actually has its origins in ancient China. "Sakura, Sakura" was performed on instruments such as the **koto**, a 13-string instrument that is more than 4000 years old, and the **shakuhachi** or bamboo flute. The unique sound of this ancient Japanese melody results from the pentatonic (or five-note) sequence used in this tonal system.

77. SAKURA, SAKURA – Band Arrangement

Japanese Folk Song
Arr. by John Higgins

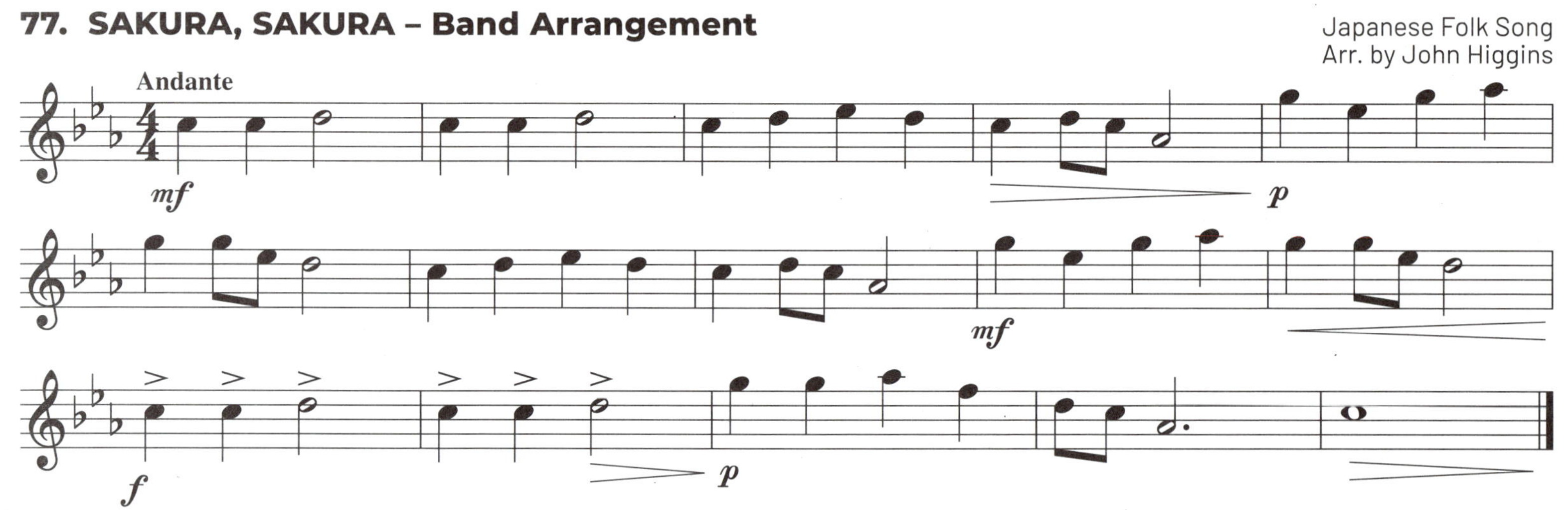

78. UP ON A HOUSETOP

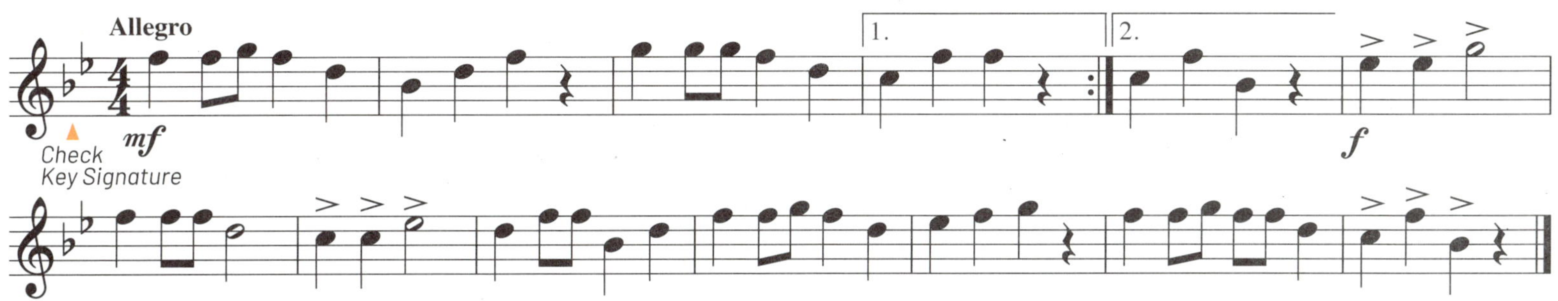

79. JOLLY OLD ST. NICK – Duet

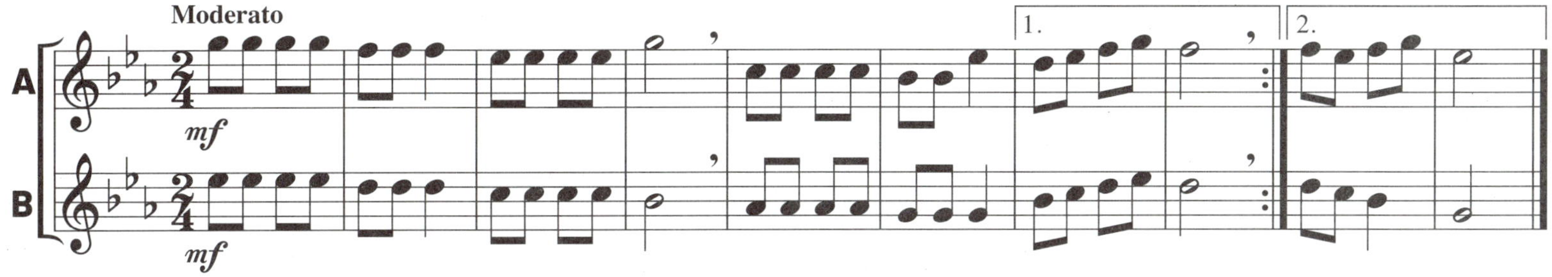

See page 9 for additional holiday music, MY DREYDL and JINGLE BELLS.

80. THE BIG AIRSTREAM – New Note

81. WALTZ THEME (THE MERRY WIDOW WALTZ)

Franz Lehar

82. AIR TIME

83. DOWN BY THE STATION

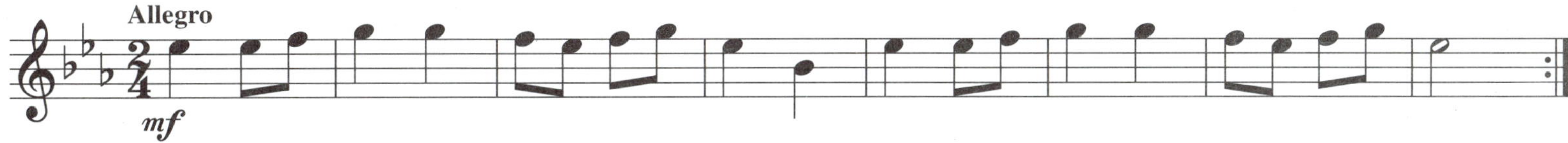

84. ESSENTIAL ELEMENTS QUIZ

85. ESSENTIAL CREATIVITY *Using these notes, improvise your own rhythms:*

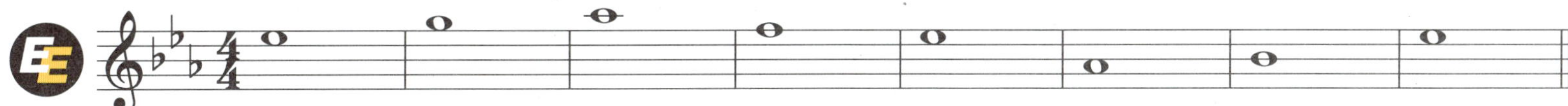

DAILY WARM-UPS

WORK-OUTS FOR TONE & TECHNIQUE

86. TONE BUILDER *Use a steady stream of air.*

87. RHYTHM BUILDER

88. TECHNIQUE TRAX

89. CHORALE *(Adapted from Cantata 147)*

Johann Sebastian Bach

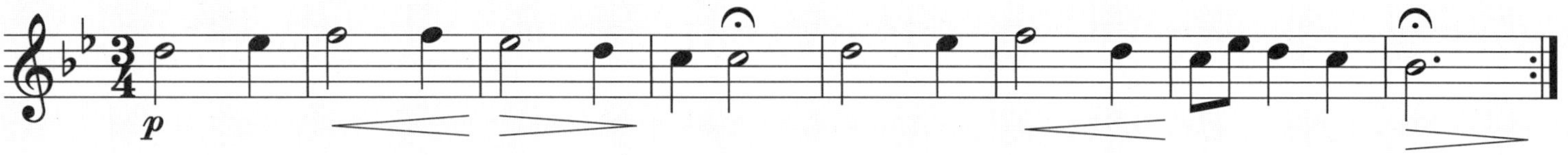

THEORY

Theme and Variations

A musical form featuring a **theme**, or primary melody, followed by **variations**, or altered versions of the theme.

90. VARIATIONS ON A FAMILIAR THEME

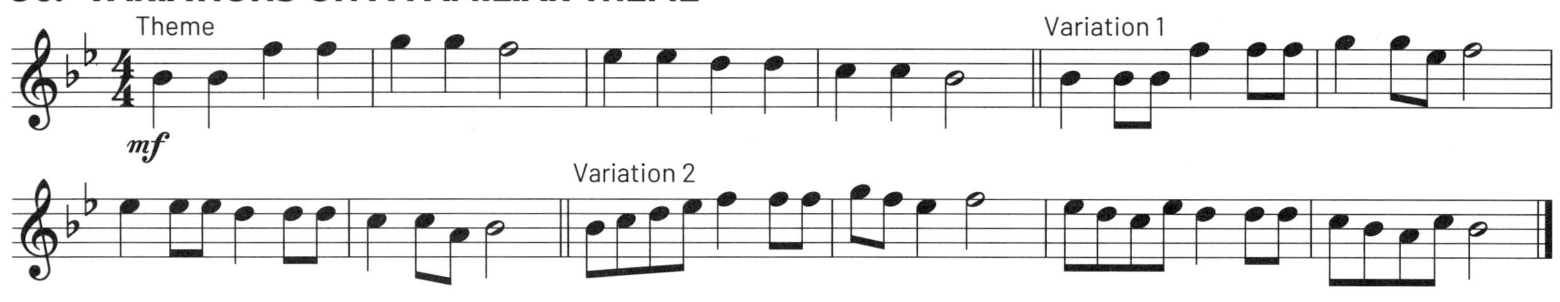

D.C. al Fine

At the **D.C. al Fine** play again from the beginning, stopping at **Fine** *(fee'- nay)*. **D.C.** is the abbreviation for **Da Capo**, or "to the beginning," and **Fine** means "the end."

91. BANANA BOAT SONG

Caribbean Folk Song

Natural ♮

A **natural** sign cancels a flat (♭) or sharp (♯) and remains in effect for the entire measure.

THEORY

92. RAZOR'S EDGE – New Note

93. THE MUSIC BOX

African-American spirituals originated in the 1700's, midway through the period of slavery in the United States. One of the largest categories of true American folk music, these primarily religious songs were sung and passed on for generations without being written down. The first collection of spirituals was published in 1867, four years after The Emancipation Proclamation was signed into law.

HISTORY

94. EZEKIEL SAW THE WHEEL

African-American Spiritual

Slur  A curved line which connects notes of different pitch. Tongue only the first note in a **slur**.

95. SMOOTH OPERATOR

▲ *Slur 2 notes – tongue only the first.*

96. GLIDING ALONG

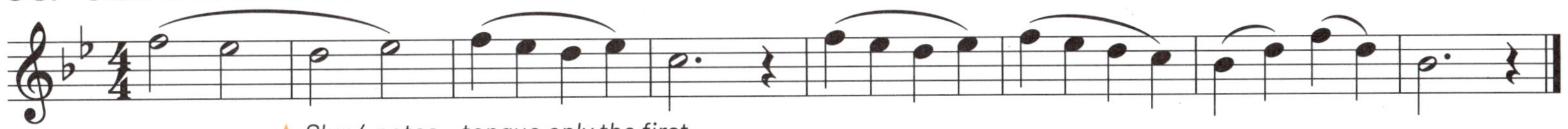

▲ *Slur 4 notes – tongue only the first.*

Ragtime is an American music style that was popular from the 1890's until the time of World War I. This early form of jazz brought fame to pianists like "Jelly Roll" Morton and Scott Joplin, who wrote "The Entertainer" and "Maple Leaf Rag." Surprisingly, the style was incorporated into some orchestral music by Igor Stravinsky and Claude Debussy. The trombones now learn to play a *glissando*, a technique used in ragtime and other styles of music.

HISTORY

97. TROMBONE RAG

98. ESSENTIAL ELEMENTS QUIZ

99. TAKE THE LEAD – New Note

THEORY

Phrase

A musical "sentence" which is often 2 or 4 measures long. Try to play a **phrase** in one breath.

100. THE COLD WIND

101. PHRASEOLOGY *Write in the breath mark(s) between the phrases.*

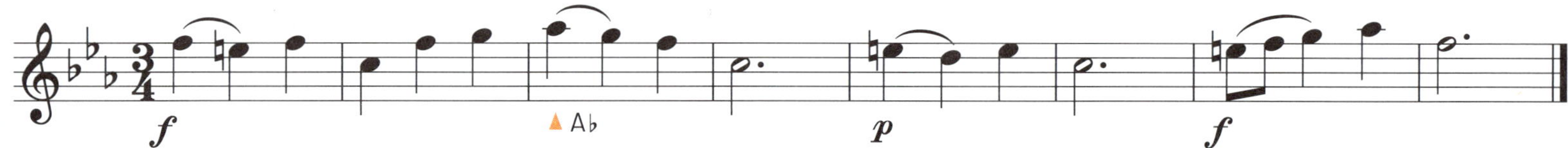

THEORY

New Key Signature

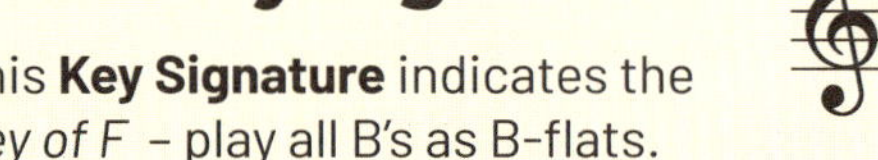

This **Key Signature** indicates the *Key of F* – play all B's as B-flats.

Multiple Measure Rest

The number above the staff tells you how many full measures to rest.
Count each measure of rest in sequence:

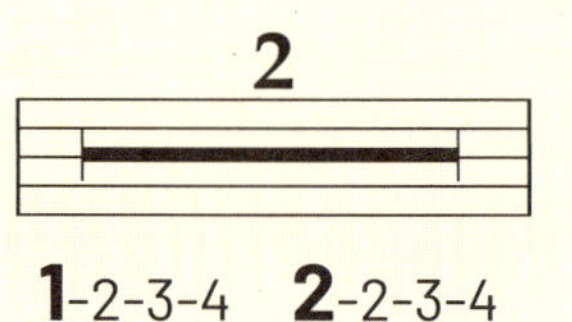

1-2-3-4 **2**-2-3-4

102. SATIN LATIN

HISTORY

German composer **Johann Sebastian Bach** (1685–1750) was part of a large family of famous musicians and became the most recognized composer of the Baroque era. Beginning as a choir member, Bach soon became an organist, a teacher, and a prolific composer, writing more than 600 masterworks. This *Minuet*, or dance in 3/4 time, was written as a teaching piece for use with an early form of the piano.

103. MINUET – Duet

Johann Sebastian Bach

104. ESSENTIAL CREATIVITY *This melody can be played in 3/4 or 4/4. Pencil in either time signature, draw the bar lines and play. Now erase the bar lines and try the other time signature. Do the phrases sound different?*

105. NATURALLY

> **HISTORY**
>
> Austrian composer **Franz Peter Schubert** (1797–1828) lived a shorter life than any other great composer, but he created an incredible amount of music: more than 600 art-songs (concert music for voice and accompaniment), ten symphonies, chamber music, operas, choral works and piano pieces. His "March Militaire" was originally a piano duet.

106. MARCH MILITAIRE – New Note

Franz Schubert

107. THE FLAT ZONE – New Note

108. ON TOP OF OLD SMOKEY

American Folk Song

> **HISTORY**
>
> **Boogie-woogie** is a style of the **blues**, and it was first recorded by pianist Clarence "Pine Top" Smith in 1928, one year after Charles Lindbergh's solo flight across the Atlantic. A form of jazz, blues music features altered notes and is usually written in 12-measure verses, like "Bottom Bass Boogie."

109. BOTTOM BASS BOOGIE – Duet

Dotted Quarter & Eighth Notes
= 2 Beats
1 & 2 &
A **dot** adds half the value of the quarter note.
1 & 2 &
A single **eighth note** has a **flag** on the stem.
110. RHYTHM RAP
Clap
1 & 2 & 3 & 4 & 1 & 2 & 3 & 4 & 1 & 2 & 3 & 4 & 1 & 2 & 3 & 4 &
111. THE DOT ALWAYS COUNTS
1 & 2 & 3 & 4 & 1 & 2 & 3 & 4 & 1 & 2 & 3 & 4 & 1 & 2 & 3 & 4 &
112. ALL THROUGH THE NIGHT
mf
Fine
p
D.C. al Fine
113. SEA CHANTY Always use a full airstream.
English Folk Song
Moderato
f
mf
f
114. SCARBOROUGH FAIR
English Folk Song
Andante
mf
f
mf
p
115. RHYTHM RAP
Clap
1 & 2 & 3 & 4 & 1 & 2 & 3 & 4 & 1 & 2 & 3 & 4 & 1 & 2 & 3 & 4 &
116. THE TURNAROUND
1 & 2 & 3 & 4 & 1 & 2 & 3 & 4 & 1 & 2 & 3 & 4 & 1 & 2 & 3 & 4 &
117. ESSENTIAL ELEMENTS QUIZ – AULD LANG SYNE
Scottish Folk Song
Andante
mf
f
Check Rhythm

PERFORMANCE SPOTLIGHT

Solo with Piano Accompaniment

You can perform this solo with or without a piano accompanist. Play it for the band, the school or your family. It is part of **Symphony No. 9 ("From The New World")** by Czech composer **Antonin Dvorák** (1841–1904). He wrote it while visiting America in 1893, and was inspired to include melodies from American folksongs and spirituals. This is the **Largo** (or "very slow tempo") theme.

118. THEME FROM "NEW WORLD SYMPHONY"

Antonin Dvorák

Great musicians give encouragement to fellow performers. On this page, clarinetists learn their instruments' upper register in the "Grenadilla Gorilla Jumps" (named after the grenadilla wood used to make clarinets). Brass players learn lip slurs, a new warm-up pattern. The success of your band depends on everyone's effort and encouragement.

119. GRENADILLA GORILLA JUMP No. 1

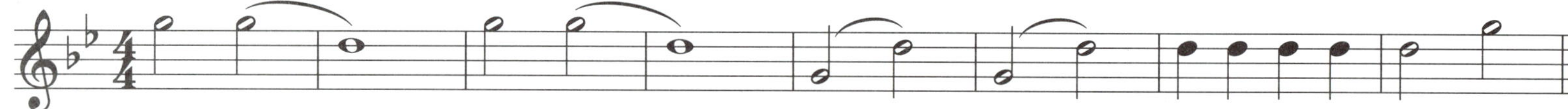

120. JUMPIN' UP AND DOWN

121. GRENADILLA GORILLA JUMP No. 2 – New Note

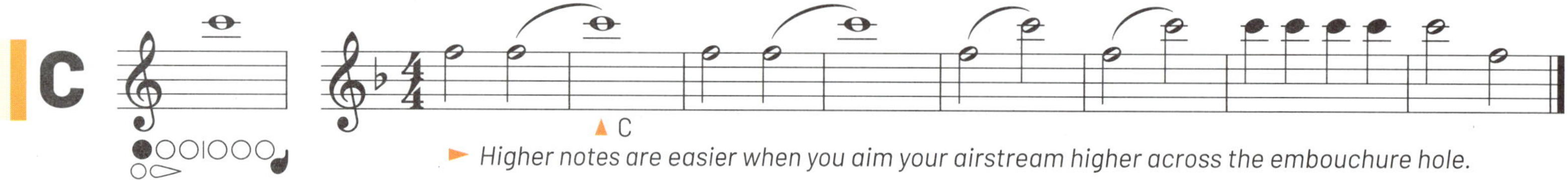

122. JUMPIN' FOR JOY

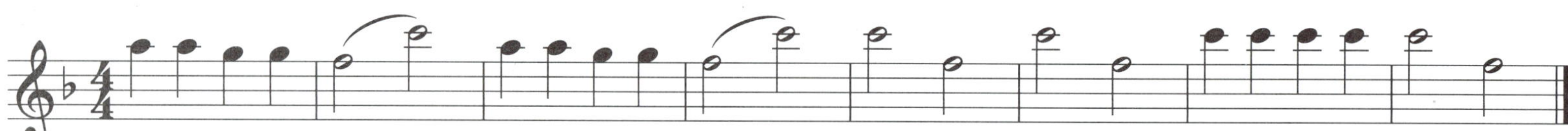

123. GRENADILLA GORILLA JUMP No. 3

124. JUMPIN' JACKS

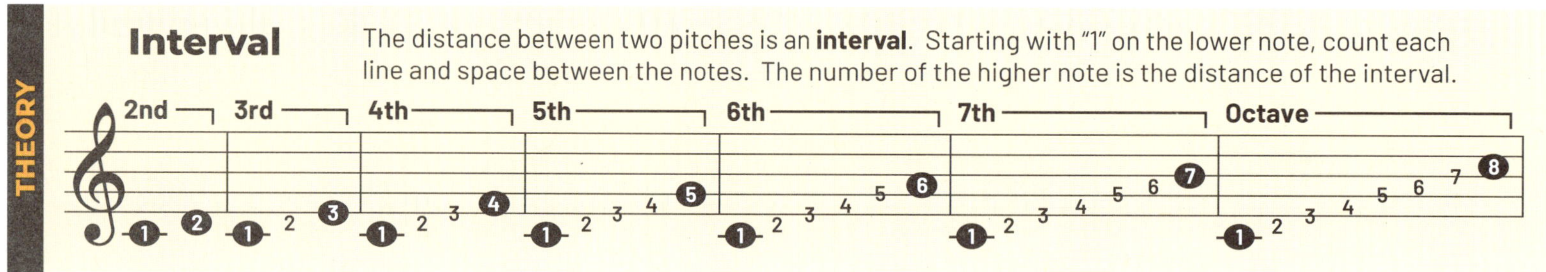

125. ESSENTIAL ELEMENTS QUIZ *Write in the numbers of the intervals, counting up from the lower notes.*

Additional bonus songs are available online. See the inside front cover for details.

126. GRENADILLA GORILLA JUMP No. 4

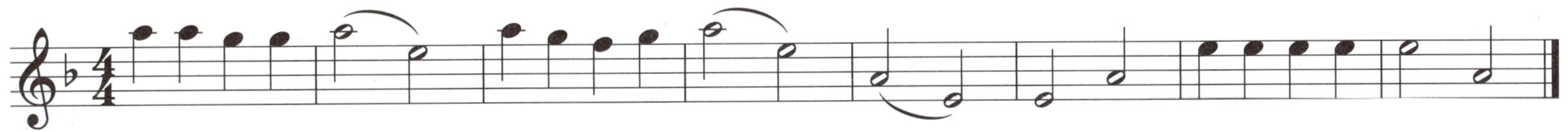

127. THREE IS THE COUNT

128. GRENADILLA GORILLA JUMP No. 5

129. TECHNIQUE TRAX

130. CROSSING OVER

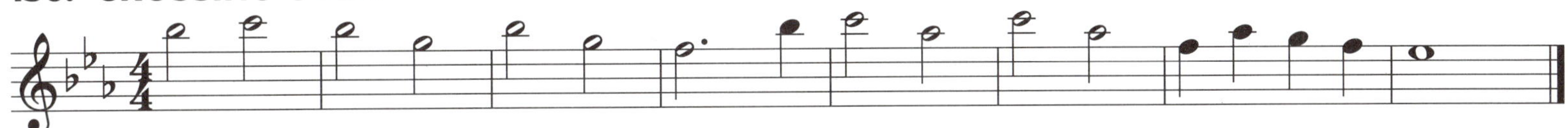

Trio A **trio** is a composition with three parts played together. Practice this trio with two other players and listen for 3-part harmony.

131. KUM BAH YAH – Trio *Always check the key signature.*

African Folk Song

Repeat Signs

Repeat the section of music enclosed by the **repeat signs**. *(If 1st and 2nd endings are used, they are played as usual – but go back only to the first repeat sign, not to the beginning.)*

132. MICHAEL ROW THE BOAT ASHORE

African-American Spiritual

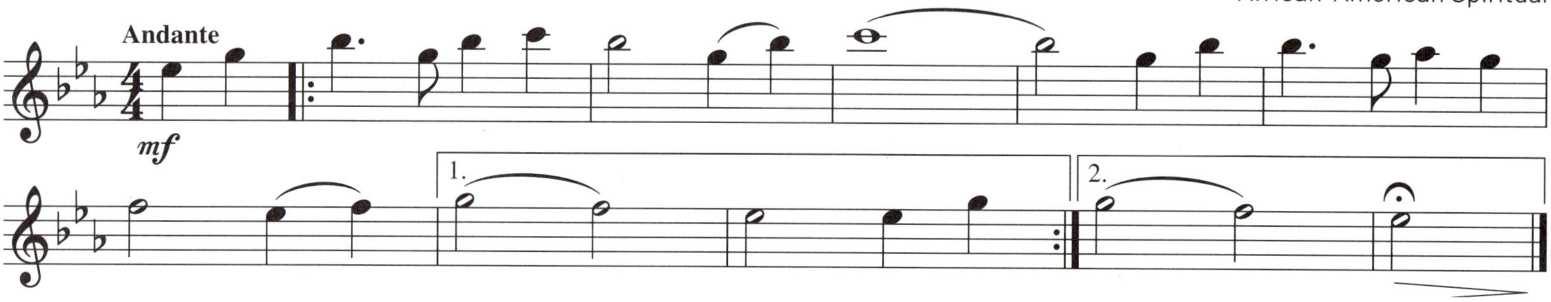

Andante

mf

1. 2.

133. AUSTRIAN WALTZ

Austrian Folk Song

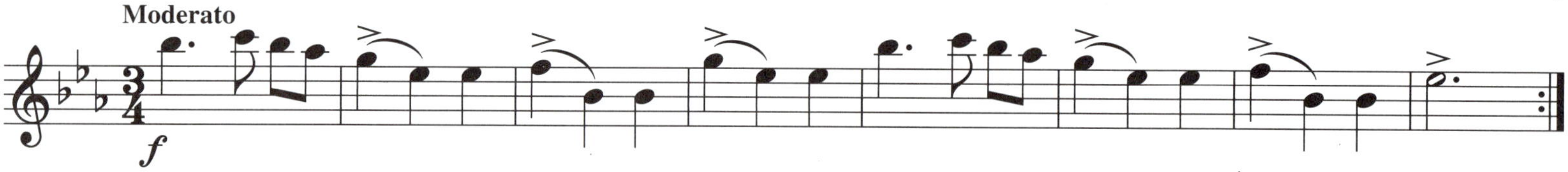

Moderato

f

134. BOTANY BAY

Australian Folk Song

Allegro

mf *f* *mf*

THEORY

C Time Signature

C = **Common Time** (Same as 4/4)

Conducting

Practice conducting this four-beat pattern.

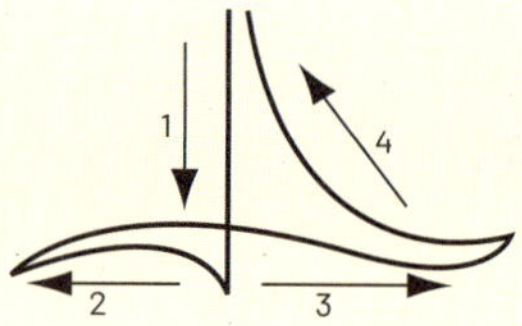

1 2 3 4

135. TECHNIQUE TRAX *Practice at all dynamic levels.*

136. FINLANDIA

Jean Sibelius

Andante

p *mf* *p*

1. 2.

137. ESSENTIAL CREATIVITY

Create your own variations by penciling in a dot and a flag to change the rhythm of any measure from ♩ ♩ *to* ♩. ♪

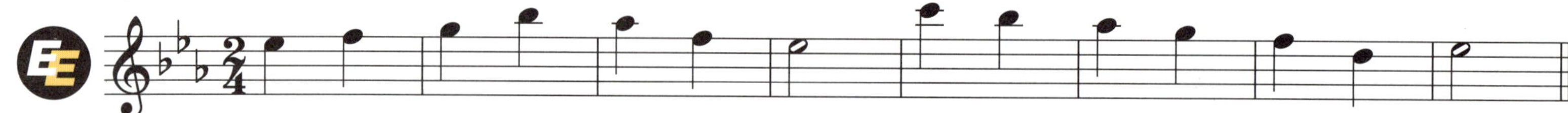

138. EASY GORILLA JUMPS

139. TECHNIQUE TRAX *Always check the key signature.*

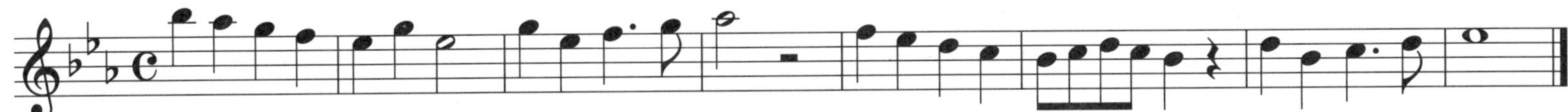

140. MORE TECHNIQUE TRAX

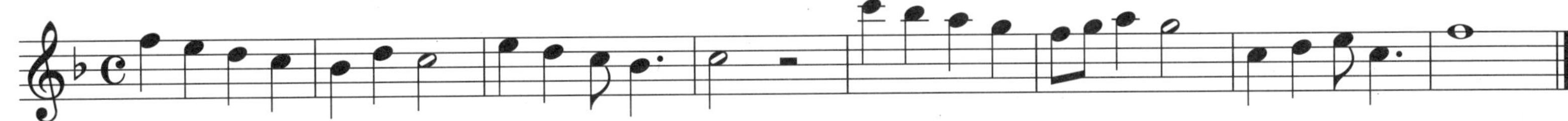

141. GERMAN FOLK SONG

142. THE SAINTS GO MARCHIN' AGAIN

143. LOWLAND GORILLA WALK

144. SMOOTH SAILING

145. MORE GORILLA JUMPS

146. FULL COVERAGE

THEORY

Scale

A **scale** is a sequence of notes in ascending or descending order. Like a musical "ladder," each step is the next consecutive note in the key. This scale is in your Key of B♭ (two flats), so the top and bottom notes are both B♭'s. The interval between the B♭'s is an octave.

147. CONCERT B♭ SCALE

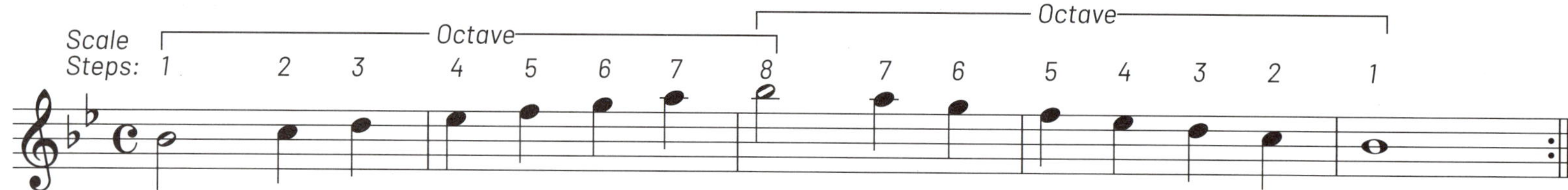

THEORY

Chord & Arpeggio

When two or more notes are played together, they form a **chord** or **harmony**. This B♭ chord is built from the 1st, 3rd and 5th steps of the B♭ scale. The 8th step is the same as the 1st, but it is an octave higher. An **arpeggio** is a "broken" chord whose notes are played individually.

148. IN HARMONY

Divide the notes of the chords between band members and play together. Does the arpeggio sound like a chord?

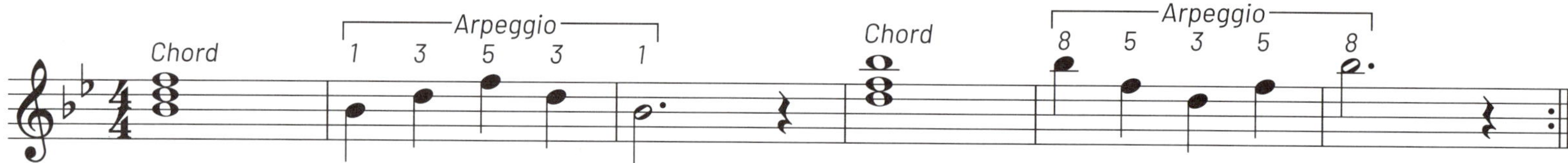

149. SCALE AND ARPEGGIO

HISTORY

Austrian composer **Franz Josef Haydn** (1732–1809) wrote 104 symphonies. Many of these works had nicknames and included brilliant, unique effects for their time. His *Symphony No. 94* was named "The Surprise Symphony" because the soft second movement included a sudden loud dynamic, intended to wake up an often sleepy audience. Pay special attention to dynamics when you play this famous theme.

150. THEME FROM "SURPRISE SYMPHONY"

Franz Josef Haydn

151. ESSENTIAL ELEMENTS QUIZ – THE STREETS OF LAREDO

American Folk Song

Write in the note names before you play.

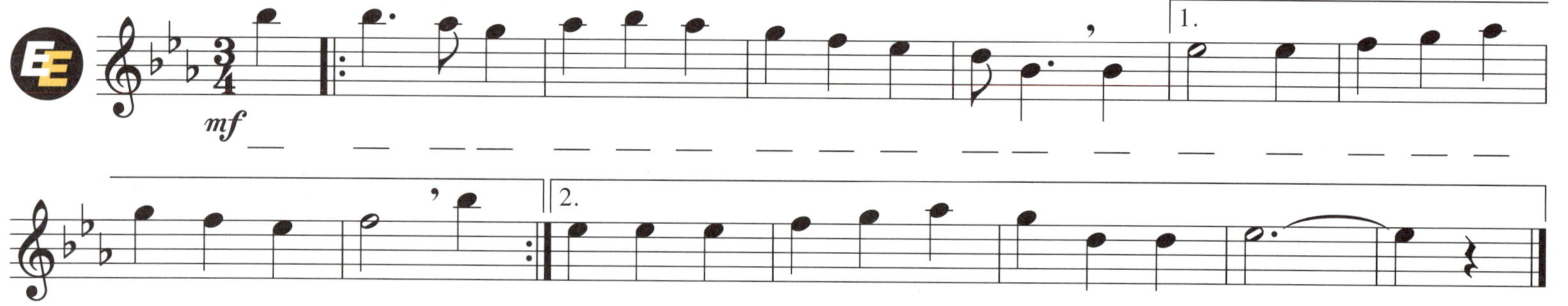

PERFORMANCE SPOTLIGHT

152. SCHOOL SPIRIT – Band Arrangement

W.T. Purdy
Arr. by John Higgins

March Style
5
Measure Number
13
21
29
1.
2.

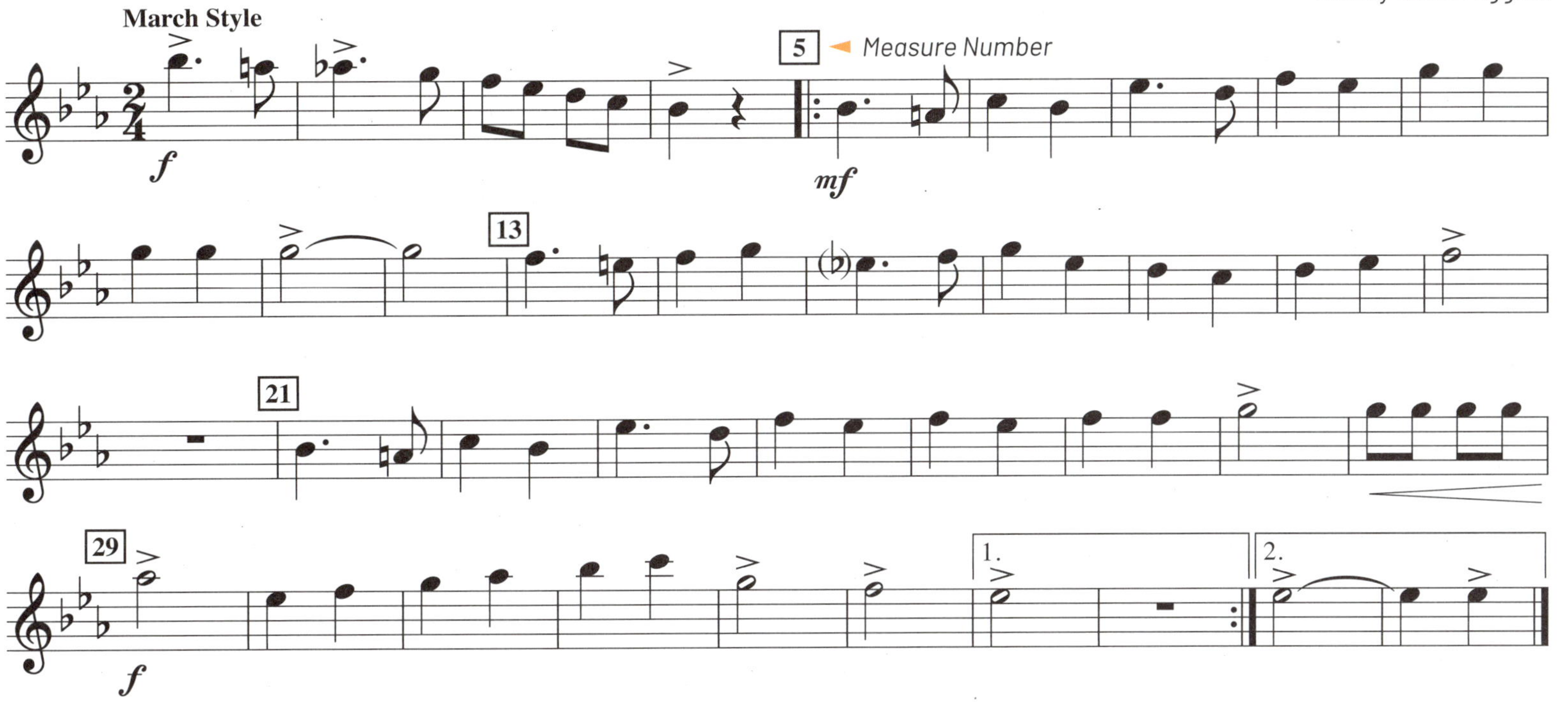

Soli When playing music marked **Soli**, you are part of a group "solo" or group feature. Listen carefully in "Carnival of Venice," and name the instruments that play the Soli part at each indicated measure number.

153. CARNIVAL OF VENICE – Band Arrangement

Julius Benedict
Arr. by John Higgins

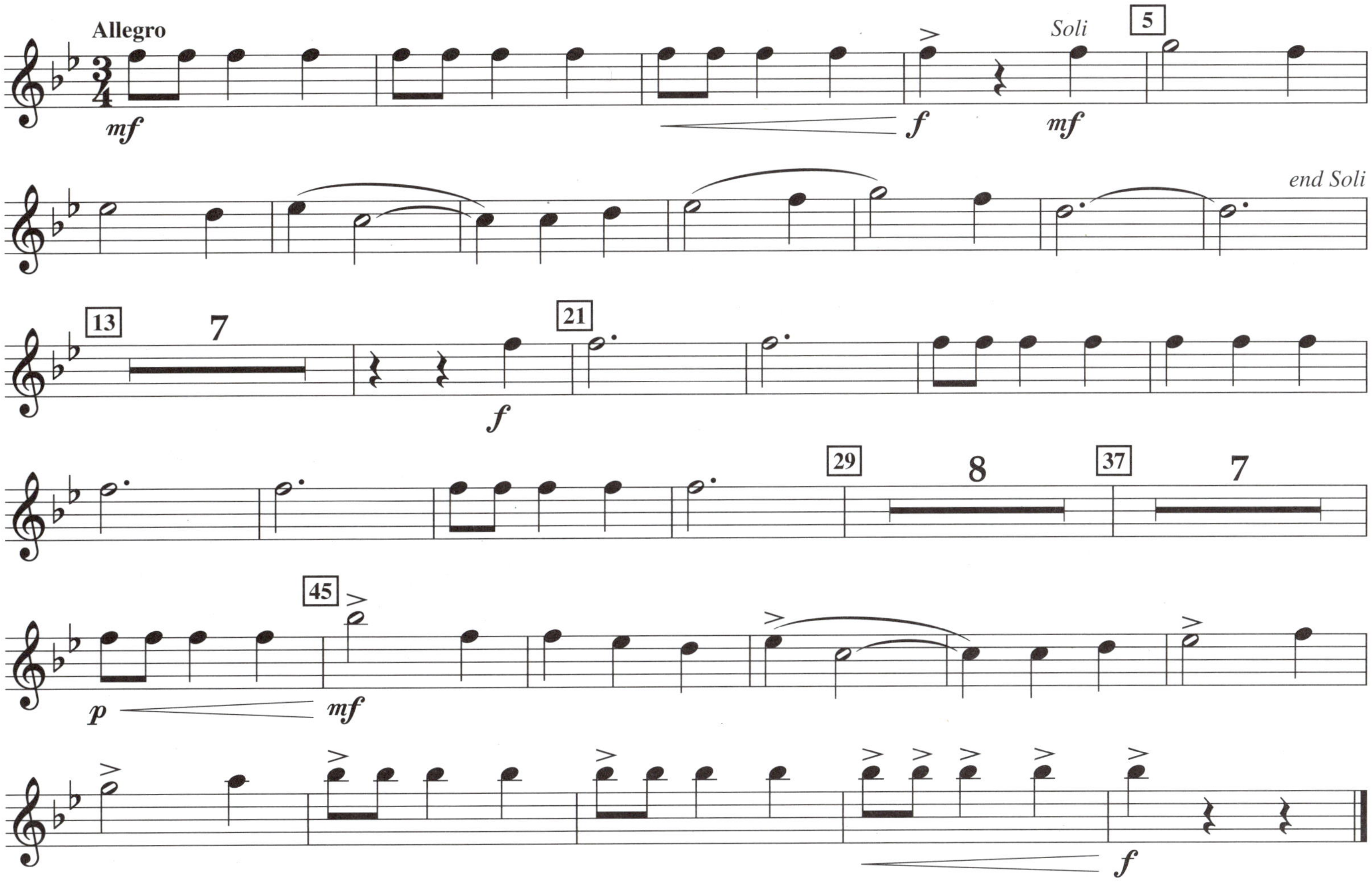

Allegro
Soli
5
end Soli
13
7
21
29
8
37
7
45

DAILY WARM-UPS

WORK-OUTS FOR TONE & TECHNIQUE

154. RANGE AND FLEXIBILITY BUILDER

155. TECHNIQUE TRAX

156. CHORALE

Johann Sebastian Bach

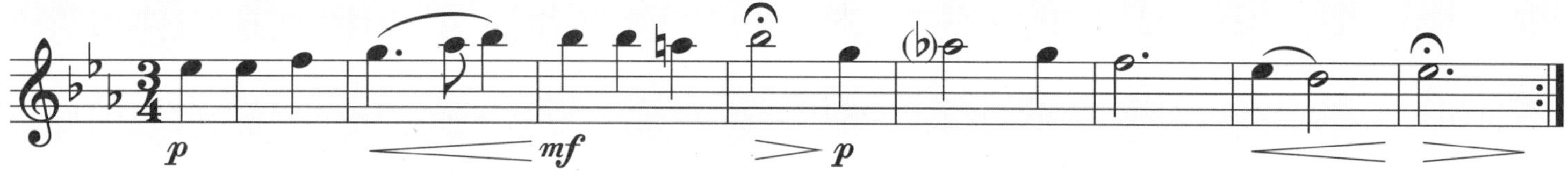

HISTORY

The traditional Hebrew melody "Hatikvah" has been Israel's national anthem since the nation's inception. At the Declaration of State in 1948, it was sung by the gathered assembly during the opening ceremony and played by members of the Palestine Symphony Orchestra at its conclusion.

157. HATIKVAH

Israeli National Anthem

Eighth Note & Eighth Rest

♪ = 1/2 beat of sound

𝄾 = 1/2 beat of silence

1 & 2 &   1 & 2 &

158. RHYTHM RAP

159. EIGHTH NOTE MARCH

160. MINUET

Johann Sebastian Bach

161. RHYTHM RAP

162. EIGHTH NOTES OFF THE BEAT

163. EIGHTH NOTE SCRAMBLE

164. ESSENTIAL ELEMENTS QUIZ

165. DANCING MELODY – New Note

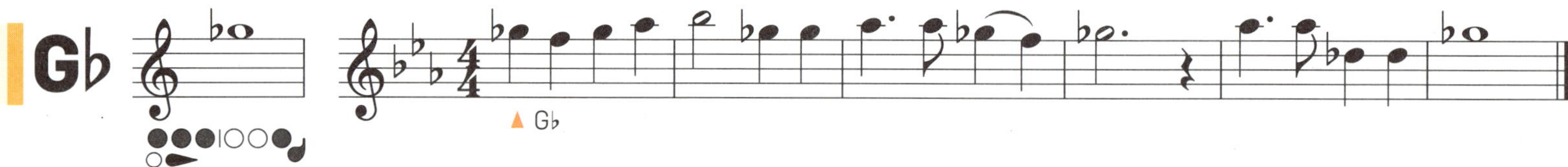

HISTORY

American composer and conductor **John Philip Sousa** (1854-1932) wrote 136 marches. Known as "The March King," Sousa wrote *The Stars And Stripes Forever*, *Semper Fidelis*, *The Washington Post* and many other patriotic works. Sousa's band performed all over the country, and his fame helped boost the popularity of bands in America. Here is a melody from his famous *El Capitan* operetta and march.

166. EL CAPITAN

John Philip Sousa

HISTORY

"O Canada," formerly known as the "National Song," was first performed during 1880 in French Canada. Robert Stanley Weir translated the English language version in 1908, but it was not adopted as the national anthem of Canada until 1980, one hundred years after its premiere.

167. O CANADA

Calixa Lavallee,
l'Hon. Judge Routhier and Justice R.S. Weir

168. ESSENTIAL ELEMENTS QUIZ – METER MANIA

Count and clap before playing. Can you conduct this?

Enharmonics

Two notes that are written differently, but sound the same (and played with the same fingering) are called **enharmonics**. Your fingering chart on pages 46–47 shows the fingerings for the enharmonic notes on your instrument.

On a piano keyboard, each black key is both a flat and a sharp:

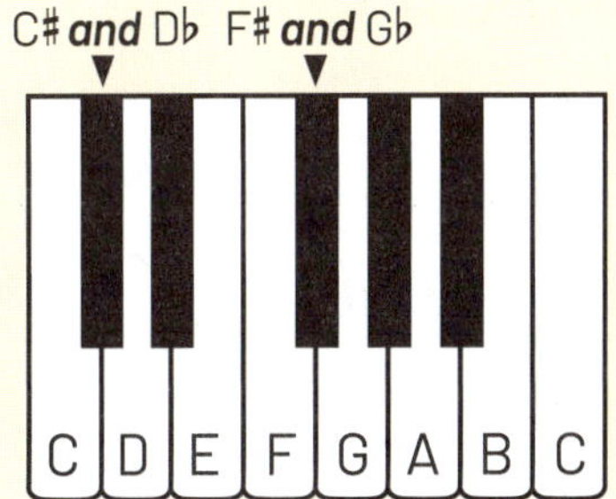

THEORY

169. SNAKE CHARMER

Enharmonic notes use the same fingering.

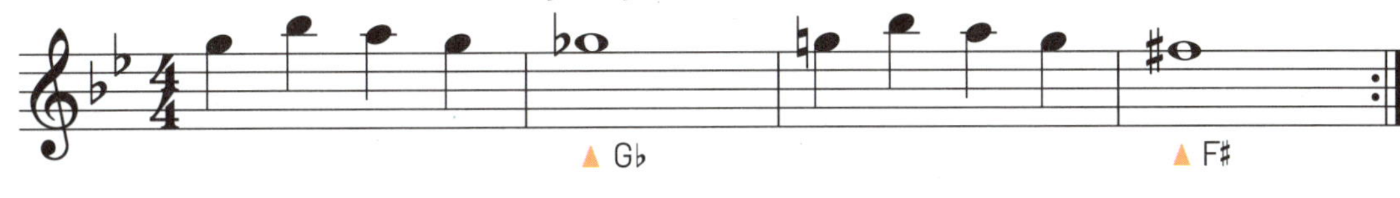

170. DARK SHADOWS

171. CLOSE ENCOUNTERS

Enharmonic notes use the same fingering.

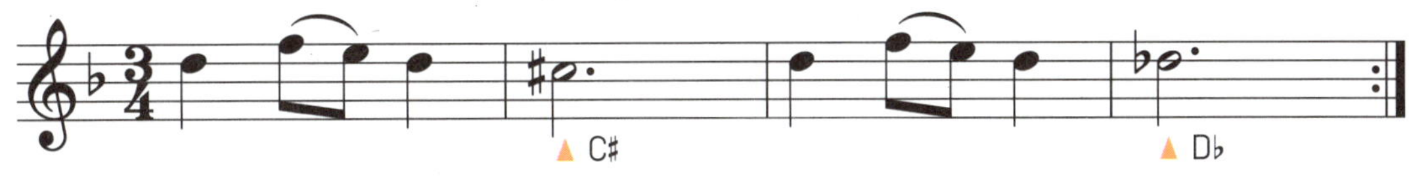

172. MARCH SLAV

173. NOTES IN DISGUISE

Chromatic Notes

Chromatic notes are altered with sharps, flats and natural signs which are not in the key signature. The smallest distance between two notes is a half-step, and a scale made up of consecutive half-steps is called a **chromatic scale**.

THEORY

174. HALF-STEPPIN'

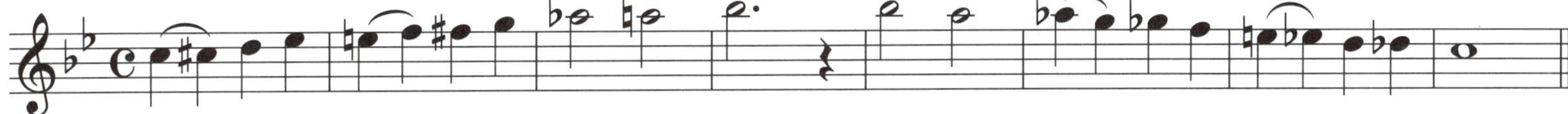

HISTORY

French composer **Camille Saint-Saëns** (1835-1921) wrote music for virtually every medium: operas, suites, symphonies and chamber works. The "Egyptian Dance" is one of the main themes from his famous opera *Samson et Delilah*. The opera was written in the same year that Thomas Edison invented the phonograph—1877.

175. EGYPTIAN DANCE *Watch for enharmonics.*

Camille Saint-Saëns

176. SILVER MOON BOAT

Chinese Folk Song

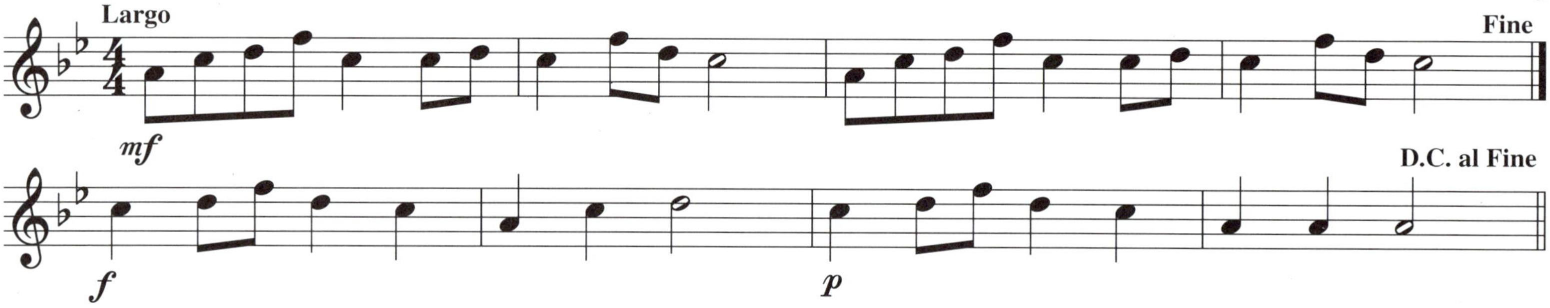

HISTORY

German composer **Ludwig van Beethoven** (1770-1827) is considered to be one of the world's greatest composers, despite becoming completely deaf in 1802. Although he could not hear his music the way we can, he could "hear" it in his mind. As a testament to his greatness, his *Symphony No. 9* (p. 13) was performed as the finale to the ceremony celebrating the reunification of Germany in 1990. This is the theme from his *Symphony No. 7*, second movement.

177. THEME FROM SYMPHONY NO. 7 – Duet

Ludwig van Beethoven

HISTORY

Russian composer **Peter Ilyich Tchaikovsky** (1840–1893) wrote six symphonies and hundreds of other works including *The Nutcracker* ballet. He was a master at writing brilliant settings of folk music, and his original melodies are among the most popular of all time. His *1812 Overture* and *Capriccio Italien* were both written in 1880, the year after Thomas Edison developed the practical electric light bulb.

Additional bonus songs are available online. See the inside front cover for details.

PERFORMANCE SPOTLIGHT

182. AMERICA THE BEAUTIFUL – Band Arrangement

Samuel A. Ward
Arr. by John Higgins

Maestoso 2 *f* 7 Andante 3 *p* 15 *f* *mf* *f* 25 Maestoso 2 *f*

183. LA CUCARACHA – Band Arrangement

Latin American Folk Song
Arr. by John Higgins

Latin Rock *f* 5 *mf* 13 *p* 25 *f* 1. 2.

PERFORMANCE SPOTLIGHT

184. THEME FROM 1812 OVERTURE – Band Arrangement

Peter Ilyich Tchaikovsky
Arr. by John Higgins

Allegro

f

p *f* *p*

10

18

mf *f*

26

34

42

PERFORMANCE SPOTLIGHT

Solo with Piano Accompaniment

Performing for an audience is an exciting part of being involved in music. This solo is based on *Serenade in G Major*, K. 525, also known as "Eine Kleine Nachtmusik" ("A Little Night Music"). **Wolfgang Amadeus Mozart** wrote this piece in 1787, the same year the American Constitution was signed into law. You and a piano accompanist can perform this for the band or at other school and community events.

185. EINE KLEINE NACHTMUSIK – Solo *(Concert E♭ version)*

Wolfgang Amadeus Mozart
Arr. by John Higgins

DUETS

Here is an opportunity to get together with a friend and enjoy playing music. The other player does not have to play the same instrument as you. Try to exactly match each other's rhythm, pitch and tone quality. Eventually, it may begin to sound like the two parts are being played by one person! Later, try switching parts.

RUBANK® SCALE AND ARPEGGIO STUDIES

KEY OF B♭ *In this key signature, play all B♭'s and E♭'s.*

KEY OF E♭ *In this key signature, play all B♭'s, E♭'s and A♭'s.*

RUBANK® SCALE AND ARPEGGIO STUDIES

KEY OF F *In this key signature, play all B♭'s.*

RHYTHM STUDIES

RHYTHM STUDIES

CREATING MUSIC

THEORY

Composition

Composition is the art of writing original music. A composer often begins by creating a melody made up of individual **phrases**, like short musical "sentences." Some melodies have phrases that seem to answer or respond to "question" phrases, as in Beethoven's *Ode To Joy*. Play this melody and listen to how phrases 2 and 4 give slightly different answers to the same question (phrases 1 and 3).

1. ODE TO JOY

Ludwig van Beethoven

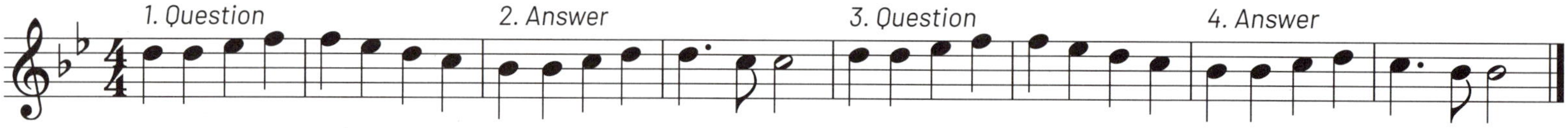

1. Question *2. Answer* *3. Question* *4. Answer*

2. Q. AND A. *Write your own "answer" phrases in this melody.*

1. Question *2. Answer*

3. Question *4. Answer*

3. PHRASE BUILDERS *Write 4 different phrases using the rhythms below each staff.*

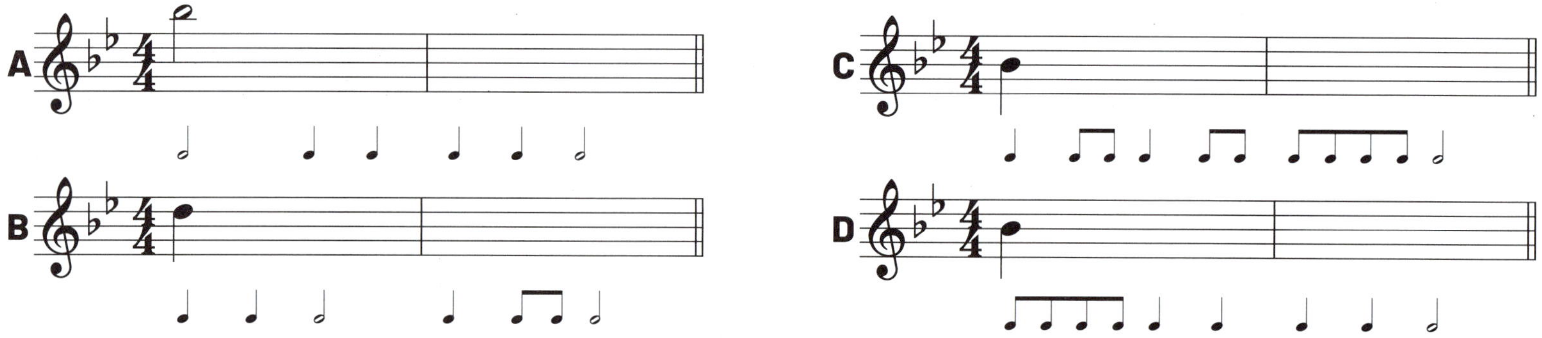

A

B

C

D

4. YOU NAME IT: ____________________

Pick phrase A, B, C, or D from above, and write it as the "Question" for phrases 1 and 3 below. Then write 2 different "Answers" for phrases 2 and 4.

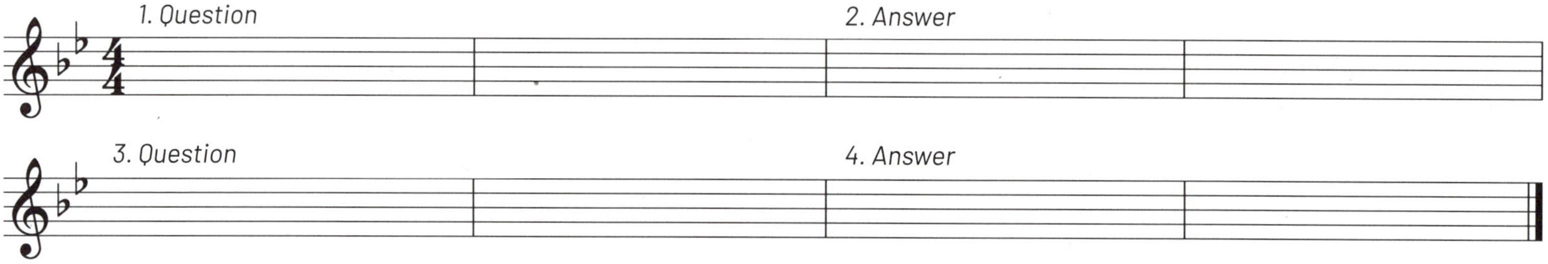

1. Question *2. Answer*

3. Question *4. Answer*

THEORY

Improvisation

Improvisation is the art of freely creating your own melody *as you play*. Use these notes to play your own melody (Line A), to go with the accompaniment (Line B).

5. INSTANT MELODY

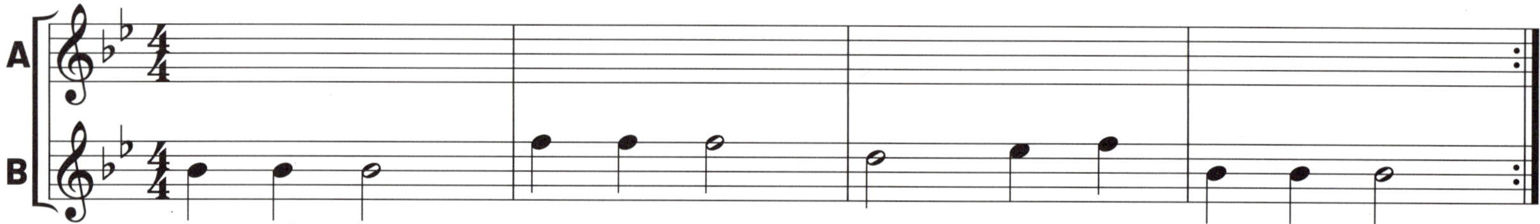

You can mark your progress through the book on this page.
Fill in the stars as instructed by your band director.

1. Page 2–3, The Basics
2. Page 5, EE Quiz, No. 13
3. Page 6, EE Quiz, No. 19
4. Page 7, EE Quiz, No. 26
5. Page 8, EE Quiz, No. 32
6. Page 10, EE Quiz, No. 45
7. Page 12–13, Performance Spotlight
8. Page 14, EE Quiz, No. 65
9. Page 15, Essential Creativity, No. 72
10. Page 17, EE Quiz, No. 84
11. Page 17, Essential Creativity, No. 85
12. Page 19, EE Quiz, No. 98
13. Page 20, Essential Creativity, No. 104
14. Page 21, No. 109
15. Page 22, EE Quiz, No. 117
16. Page 23, Performance Spotlight
17. Page 24, EE Quiz, No. 125
18. Page 26, Essential Creativity, No. 137
19. Page 28, No. 149
20. Page 28, EE Quiz, No. 151
21. Page 29, Performance Spotlight
22. Page 31, EE Quiz, No. 164
23. Page 32, EE Quiz, No. 168
24. Page 33, No. 174
25. Page 35, EE Quiz, No. 181
26. Page 36, Performance Spotlight
27. Page 37, Performance Spotlight
28. Page 38, Performance Spotlight

MUSIC — AN ESSENTIAL ELEMENT OF LIFE

FINGERING CHART

FLUTE

○ = Open

● = Pressed down

The most common fingering appears first when two fingerings are shown.

Instrument Care Reminders

Before putting your instrument back in its case after playing, do the following:

- Carefully remove the head joint.
- Put a clean soft cloth on the end of your cleaning rod and swab out the head joint.
- Twist the middle and foot joints apart and draw the cleaning rod through each joint.
- Carefully wipe the outside of each section to keep the finish clean.

Instruments and photos courtesy of Yamaha.

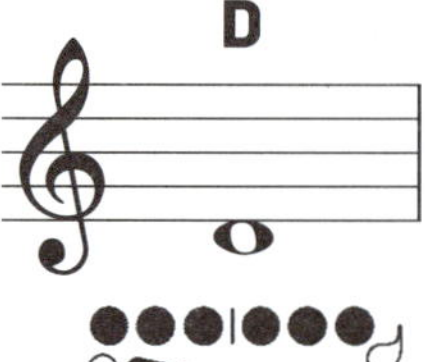

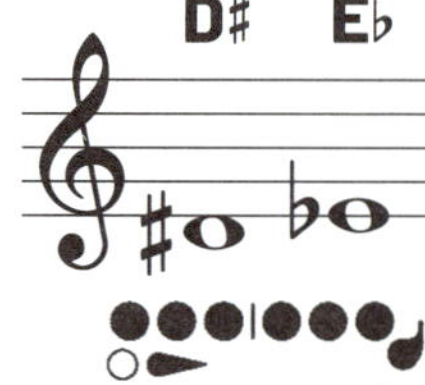

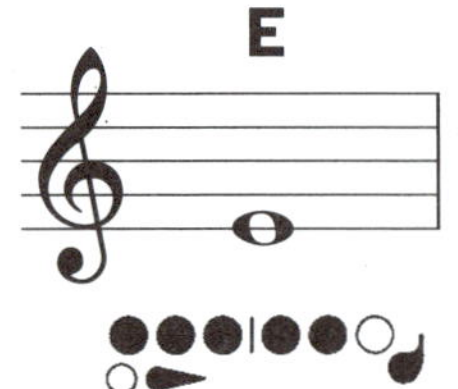

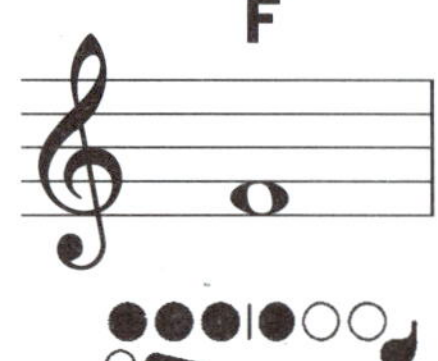

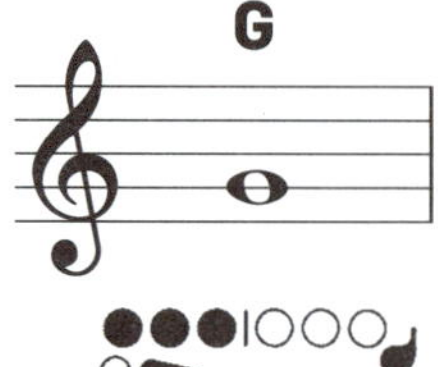

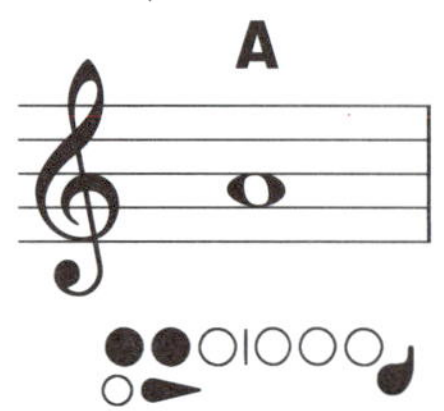

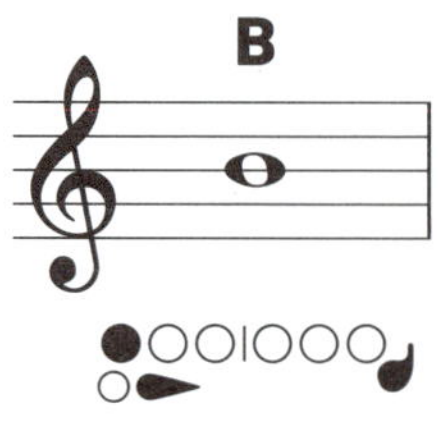

FINGERING CHART

FLUTE

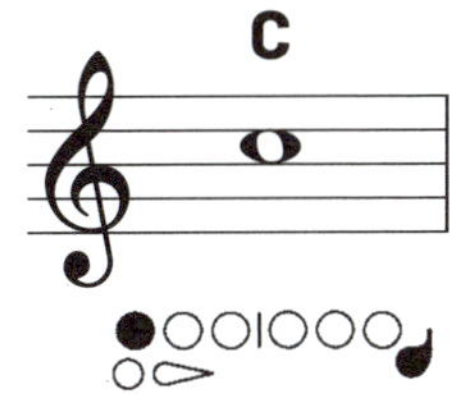

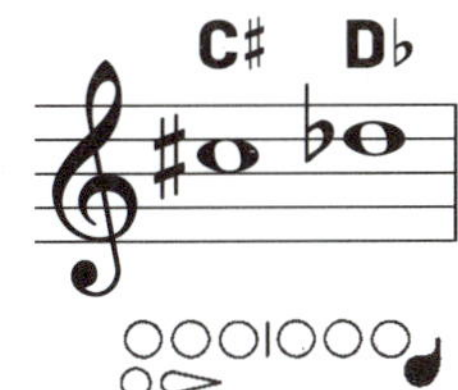

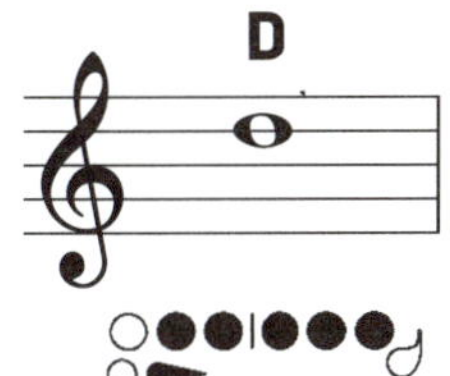

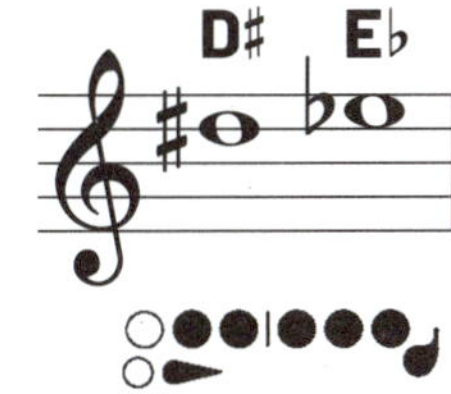

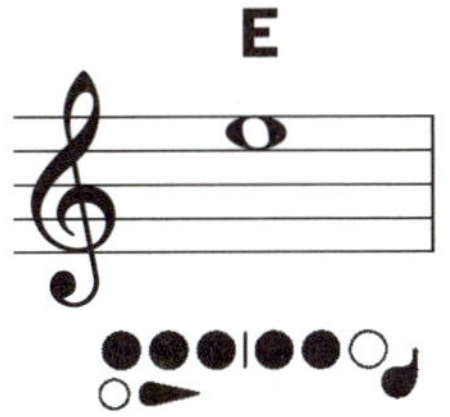

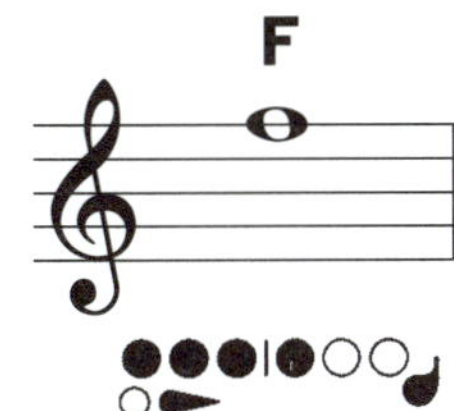

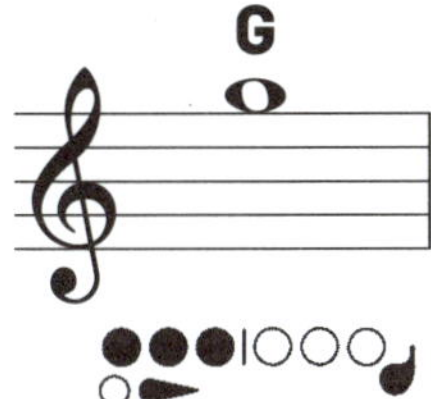

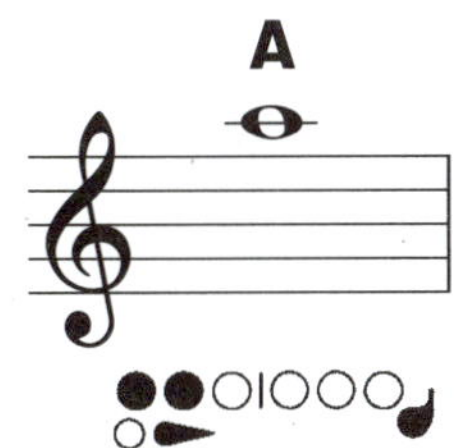

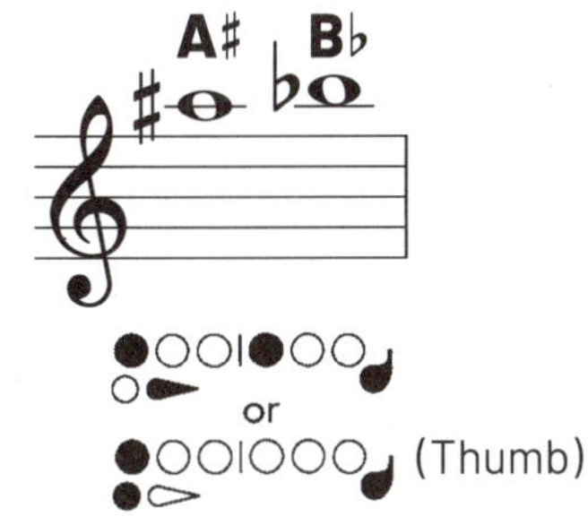

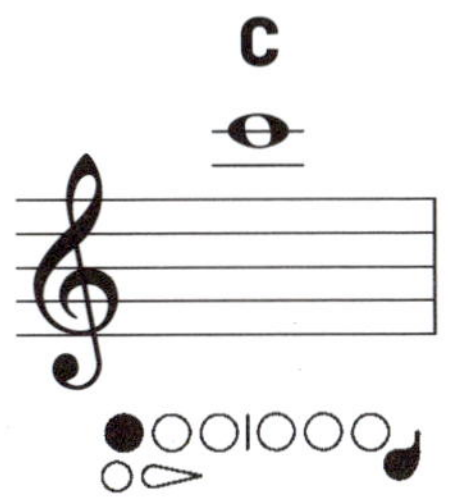

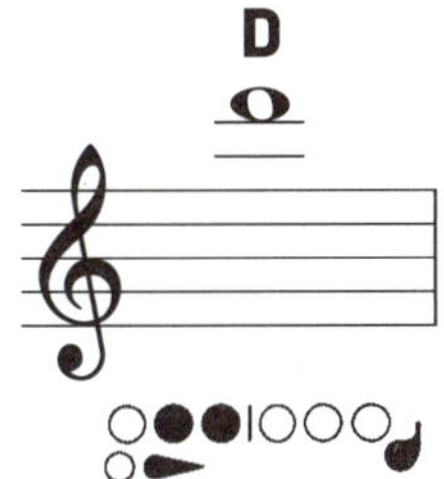

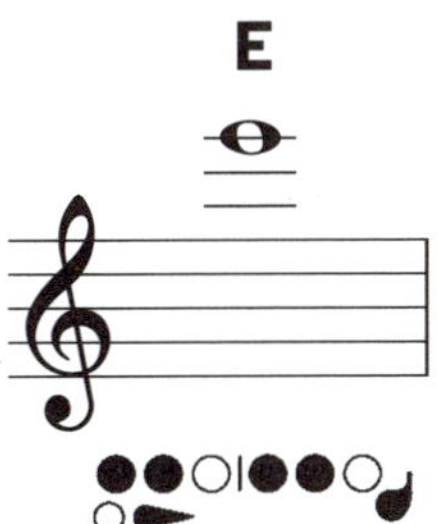

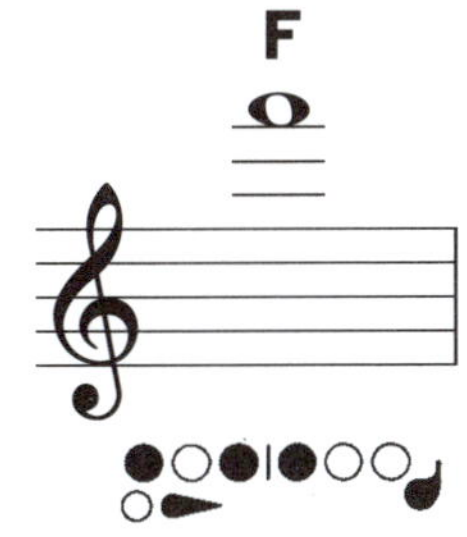

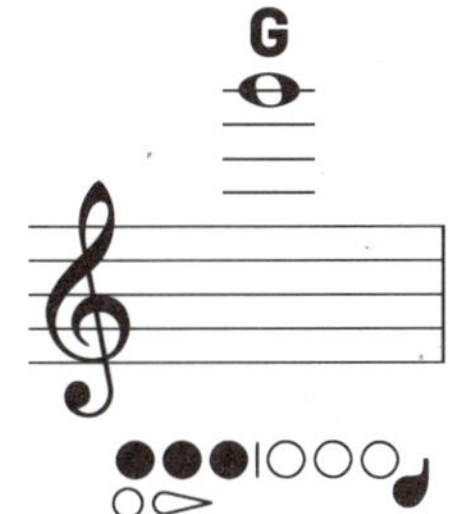

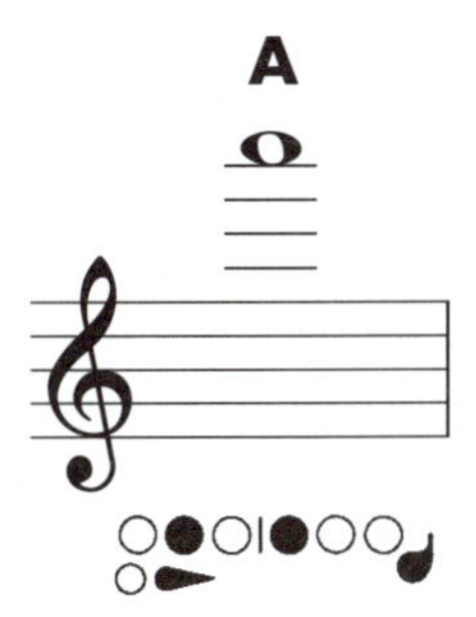

Reference Index

Definitions (pg.)

Composers

World Music